Mayakovsky and Stalin

Mayakovsky and Stalin

Murray Mednick

PADUA
PLAYWRIGHTS
PRODUCTION

Padua Playwrights Press, Los Angeles

Editorial director: Dan Tucker
Cover design: Brian McWilliams
Interior template: CoDe. New York Inc., Jenny 8 del Corte Hirschfeld
and Mischa Leiner
Supervising Padua editor: Guy Zimmerman

All inquiries, including requests for permission for the plays contained herein,
should be directed to:

Guy Zimmerman
Padua Playwrights Productions
840 Micheltorena Street
Los Angeles CA 90026

Printed in the United States of America

Distributed in the United States and Canada by Theater Communications Group,
520 Eighth Avenue, 24th Floor, New York, NY 10018-4156
ISBN: 9780990725633

Contents

Introduction

1.

Murray Mednick's *Mayakovsky and Stalin* is a play about the toll political history takes on the poetic sensibility; *Mayakovsky and Stalin* is also a play about the idiotic redundancies of despotic power. Scenes between Vladimir Mayakovsky and the actress Lily Brik alternate with scenes between Joseph Stalin and his second wife Nadja as both couples navigate the turbulence of Russia in the late 1920s and '30s. Determined to love outside of prescribed marital norms, Volodya and Lilyana embody the vanguard idealism of the Revolution of 1917. Stalin and Nadja, meanwhile, live at the pinnacle of the emerging Soviet state as it reveals itself to be as brutal as anything it replaced. This revelation triggers the two suicides that bookend *Mayakovsky and Stalin*—at the open Nadja kills herself with a bullet to the heart. The text then flashes back in time, tracking its characters through the 1917 Revolution and what came after. The play concludes with Mayakovsky's self-administered shot to the heart (like Nadja he uses a Mauser for the job.)

Mednick depicts Stalin, or Koba, as he was known to his Bolshevik comrades, as canny, domineering, and ruthless. Seizing control after Lenin's death in 1924 Stalin became the "man of steel"—Koba means "steel" in Russian—who would forge the new Communist order. With its pre-industrial peasant economy, Czarist Russia had always been a most unlikely arena for a Marxist revolution. Stalin had an answer for that, just as he had an answer for everything, a confidence that led to the massive purges of the 1930s. Stalin's presence in the play is immediate and compelling. We meet Koba enjoying leisure time, hunting in the company of terrified underlings and lackeys, while also planning tactical operations in the wake of the mass collectivizations of 1929. In these brief, intricate scenes, Mednick captures the combination of decisiveness and grandiosity that made Stalin one of the most dangerous men of the modern era.

In domestic exchanges with the articulate Nadja, Mednick gives Stalin a private voice, and alongside the addition to forceful action and despotic violence we hear also a capacity for feeling. Like so many of Stalin's victims, Nadja is a comrade committed to the cause of the revolution. When she laments his brutality, Stalin calls on her to put her squeamishness aside—they have a new world to create. Seeing through this "impeccable ideology," she points out the horror of his "just cause," which in the end boils down to a bloody totalitarian power game. Nadja knows this because, of course, the dynamic extends into their marriage as well. As his underling Kirov puts it, Stalin "is a slave to everyone around him, and everyone around him is his slave." And so, finally, Nadja picks up her Mauser and stages her own little revolution, taking her own life.

The Stalin of *Mayakovsky and Stalin* makes a perfect foil for Mayakovsky, his obdurate belief in his own righteousness providing Mednick with an armature by which to track Mayakovsky deep into his growing despair. The two men are brought into the same frame by Lily Brik's campaign to restore the dead poet's reputation as the voice of the Revolution, an idea Stalin endorses without much enthusiasm. As a Jew, Lily is especially attuned to the dark forces at work in the new Soviet society, and she recoils as Mayakovsky's vision turns toward the apocalyptic. The poet's suicide in 1930 was a harbinger of the darkness to come, the deep nihilism animating Stalin's totalitarian project leading quickly to the deaths of millions of Russians in the purges defining the decade.

A willingness to speak the truth even when it might cost him his life redeems Mayakovsky from his towering vanity. Passionate, mercurial, endlessly provocative, Mayakovsky was a public figure as well as a poet. He brought glamour and theatricality to the Revolution, and served as an exemplary figure for the new Russia. Initially delighting in the energies released by the Czarist order as it fell, Mayakovsky quickly recognized the brutality of the new regime. "We act like deranged insects" sums up his view of modern man. The poet's final scenes have an astonishing intimacy to them. His fatal gunshot is the culmination of a life spent searching for a final note, or what he calls "the exact whole moment."

Defining so clearly the end point of the play allows Mednick to focus our attention on the subtle foreshadowings and alternative pathways that attend these two reluctant martyrs—Nadja and Mayakovsky—as they move through time toward their graves. With great economy of means, Mednick captures in the play's brief, quasi-Brechtian scenes, a great arc of twentieth-century history. Power and the poetic—in Mednick's play these two forces wind around each other in amplifying spirals, delivering us finally to an indictment of human folly in its modern form. "People will do anything. In the circumstances," Mayakovsky says, cutting to the heart of the matter. "All they have to do is feel in the right." Like Shakespeare's histories, *Mayakovsky and Stalin* reminds us that, in the right hands, bringing epochal catastrophes to life is one of the things theater can do well in the right hands.

2.

Helping Mednick capture the dissolution of Russia's revolutionary dreams is his own direct experience of idealism colliding with fallen human nature. The playwright's sensibility was formed by a later episode of utopian exuberance—the counterculture of the 1960s. Born in 1939 and raised in difficult circumstances in Brooklyn and the Catskills, Mednick was a published poet by his early twenties, and a denizen of the arts scene on the Lower East Side. By 1964, he had found his way to Theatre Genesis, where his friend Sam Shepard had also begun to write plays. It is worth noting in passing that Shepard and Mayakovsky were to some extent cut from the same cloth—literary celebrities of their day who mixed authentic talent with a certain amount of showboating. (The link explains the cutting asides that pepper the narrator's commentary about Volodya, and his tone of wry exasperation at the poet's growing fame.) Along with the acerbic William Burroughs, Allen Ginsburg and Gregory Corsi were the defining figures of the literary underground of the Lower East Side, and Mednick's work retains from that era a sense that the poetic and the spiritual travel along parallel paths. Mednick's play *The Deer Kill* won an Obie award in 1970 when the cultural tide was beginning to turn. Like the revolutionary idealists of Russia, Mednick watched the fondest dreams of his generation whither and die over the next decade. The playwright moved west to Los Angeles to found the Padua Hills Playwrights Workshop/Festival (1978)–1995). Broadly speaking, the 1970s were a long transitional period, the mechanics of history tractoring forward into the conservative Reagan era and the long nightmare that has come after.

With hindsight, it becomes clear how singular the Off-Off Broadway movement was as a laboratory for bold experimentation in the art of theater. Rooted in the performative innovations of Grotowski and Brecht, this legacy is often approached through the directorial explorations of Peter Brook, Joe Chaiken and others. Less often appreciated is the contribution of poet-playwrights within the Off-Off scene—Shepard and Mednick, and also their important colleague Maria Irene Fornes. These playwrights brought Beckett into the mix to open up new arenas of practice in which forms of poetic irony are married to embodied performance. Mednick was able to continue exploring this approach to theater-making on the West Coast. His style continues to evolve through the seminal *Coyote Cycle* (1978–86), his plays with Ed Harris (*Are You Lookin?* and *Scar*), his explorations of Jewish life post-Holocaust (*Fedunn, Joe and Betty, Mrs. Feuerstein, Clown Show for Bruno*), and the avant-garde *The Gary Plays* cycle completed in 2010.

This remarkable development required a creative milieu in which the playwright could explore theatrical form directly with actors. Despite the absence of a sizeable audience for theater in Los Angeles, the city is home to a surplus of talented actors for playwrights to collaborate with, and very few producers to mess things up. Over the course of four decades, Mednick was able to continue the development of his unique approach to writing for the stage. In his later plays, Mednick's ear for the rhythms of everyday speech come to approximate the quicksilver fluidity of our feeling-thought. The flow of scenes back and forth in *Mayakovsky* is meditative in this way, carrying the audience with it in an episode of collective awareness that is rare indeed, and highly refined.

3.

In Mednick's hands, theater becomes once again essentially a literary or poetic art, the text itself providing the actor with a direct source of performative energy.

For the benefit of those contemplating producing a Mednick play—a highly recommended activity—it is worth slowing down for a moment to highlight the technical issues with staging this work.

At first glance, Mednick's plays might seem like a refined variant of dramatic realism, but while their dialogue is always rooted in how people actually speak, something quite different is at work. One rule of directing Mednick's plays is that the text always works far better if the actors "cheat" to face out. Facing in and connecting with other actors in the mode required by dramatic realism deprives the audience of a full experience of what is most significant in a poetic play—the shimmering of emotion and thought through the window of the actor's face as it is disclosed by enacting the text. This is the mode of theater-writing Mednick has raised to a high art. It is worth looking closer at what is entailed here.

In a piece of conventional dramatic realism, an actor must breathe life into prosaic exchanges that tilt strongly toward received ideas of subjectivity and of identity. The text itself lacks the living pulse of the poetic; in other words, direct interaction with other actors becomes crucial to this task. In plays rooted in the conventions of dramatic realism, actors face each other, exchanging emotional action and reaction to inform the weave of objective and obstacles that structure dramatic action. We are watching a little corner of the normative world, conceived as a stable construct deviating in large or small ways from a commonsense ideal. Accuracy of representation is the aim here, and much of the pleasure for an audience involves laying aside for a time the burdens of actual experience. We inhabit, after all, a world devoid of inherent meaning. We must create meaning out of experience, and then we must create it again. There is no stable, preexisting order for a playwright to represent, but instead a dynamic field of forces in play that requires effort and energy to navigate. This is what we encounter in a play by Mednick, and the actor must work in a different key.

In Mednick's poetic approach to theater, nothing is presupposed. Stalin and Mayakovsky exist only in how they speak, and the scenes arise from what they say, creating the world of the play. Watching the play, we engage directly with actual experience itself, with all its hidden complexities and challenges. The requirements for an actor (not to mention a director) are altogether different. The lines of a Mednick play are alive with poetic energy the actor can tap directly. Other actors doing likewise are important on the level of emotional color, timing, and tone—the musicality of the event—but not as a source of performative energy. The actor in a Mednick play, in other words, does not need to *complete* anything, because the text is already complete. She becomes more of a medium, or a sensitive musician in charge of an instrument, and the work requires the discipline and technical mastery to simply get out of the way.

As can happen performing Beckett—or Pinter, Albee, Churchill, Shawn, Fornes or Parks, or any of the other playwrights embracing this basic approach—actors in a Mednick play can sometimes feel displaced. But Mednick's approach is in fact rooted in a profound respect for what it is actors actually *do*—which is to mediate between worlds. Mednick shows his actors the respect of crafting texts that will enable them to levitate and fly, becoming an Other.

The other rules of performing Mednick fall out from this same poetic quality. With Mednick, it is almost always better for actors to move without speaking, land firmly, and then speak their lines. Embodied action here has its own poetic and formal quality, set in dynamic tension to the subtle but persistent rhythms of the language.

The silences filled with movement merge with the iambic heartbeat animating the dialogue. Without calling attention to themselves, these rhythms operate beneath the words.

It would be difficult to overstate the necessity of observing these rules, which press against the fundamental tenets of stage realism that have been dominant since Stanislavsky. Part of the impact of listening to a Mednick play is how the work cuts against the fundamental binary of mind and body, reorganizing in real time our experience of both. This is where Mednick's work announces its solidarity with that of Beckett, who revived ways to deploy irony and paradox to achieve similar aims. And yet, as innovative as this aspect of Mednick's aesthetic may seem, theater history provides obvious precedents for the approach. Shakespeare is best performed out in the same way. The Greeks too, arguably, the chorus and protagonist facing out for the crucial moments. A style of staging common to Shakespeare, Sophocles, and Beckett obviously has something to recommend it. And yet Mednick's innovations extend still further, toward a reinvention of the classical chorus.

In Mednick's plays after *Tirade for Three* (1997), there is almost always a chorus mediating between the world of the play and the world of the audience. This choral figure played a central feature of Mednick's eight-play cycle *The Gary Plays*, completed in 2010. Wry asides, vaudevillian humor, facts and figures—the choral technique gives Mednick's text amplitude and scope. These voices arose in Mednick's work as a function of what was possible in the poetic mode he had opened up. *Mayakovsky and Stalin* testifies to how Mednick's embrace of the classical chorus continues to evolve. Now a historical being, the narrator in *Mayakovsky* stands in for the author himself, directing the flow of feeling and thought back and forth through time and from place to place, tapping the full potential of the open space of the stage.

Mayakovsky and Stalin becomes stunning at its close, the playwright's mastery allowing him to tap deep feeling and to stop, if only for a moment, the rushing-on of time and the nightmare of history. As men with big, stupid ideas afflict us once again, how nice to be able to pause and take a breath, perhaps even catch a glimpse of the "whole moment" Mayakovsky wanted most of all to actualize. This forward-looking quality makes *Mayakovsky and Stalin* relevant in several ways to millennials confronting updated digitized versions of familiar demons—authoritarianism, the social violence being stoked and channeled toward visions of a new world, the desecration and destruction of the natural world at every scale. The play also reminds us that, more than any of the other Communist strongmen, Stalin fatally compromised the ideals of socialism, which today has been reduced to a historical curiosity. As we contemplate a trajectory pointing toward ever-greater disparities between rich and poor and the collapse of living systems everywhere, the discrediting of alternative modes of arranging our societies is perhaps Stalin's greatest crime against humanity.

There's something healing too in the way Mednick brings these two quasi-mythic figures down to human scale. The gorgeous rhetoric of everyday speech makes Stalin and Mayakovsky into mortal beings. In Mednick's canon they join a growing gallery that includes the poet Paul Celan, the Nazi philosopher Martin Heidegger (*G-Nome*), the writer Bruno Schulz (*Clown Show for Bruno*), and the French poet Villon (*Villon*). What unites these different texts is a poetic quality and an appreciation for the powers of formal rhetoric—look at any line in a Mednick text and you will find a quiet, understated elegance that exists alongside the shadings of character and diction. Even the slang in Mednick is perfectly phrased, every comma arriving on time and in the right place. Stalin always sounds exactly like Stalin, and Mayakovsky always speaks in the same voice, but both conform to the flawless economy of expression we associate with fine literature.

Mayakovsky and Stalin

A Play by Murray Mednick

Characters

MAYAKOVSKY (VOLODYA)   STALIN(KOBA)
LILY (Lilyana)   NADJA (Second wife)
OSIP (Lily's husband)   KIROV (Comrade)
MASHA (Maid)   ELSA (Lily's sister)
VOROSHILOV (Comrade)   CHORUS (plus KIROV and VOROSHILOV)

The set

*An historical montage of photos and film of the Soviet Union,
dating from the early 1900s to the death of Mayakovsky. The play's
characters sit upstage beneath the wall of changing images (including portraits of Stalin, Nadja, Mayakovsky, Lily and Osip Brik,
etc.), facing the audience. The actors stand or come downstage to
play their scenes, then return to their seats. Standing is an entrance,
sitting an exit.*

*Note: Dialogue in parentheses are asides or to/for themselves. Stage
directions are as usual. Lines in italics are assigned to **the chorus.***

Act 1
Scene 1

A dinner party in the Kremlin.
A gunshot blasts through the
Plated French windows.

A thump as Nadja falls to the floor.

A gunshot—the woman slumps over, the guests
stare—No, she shot herself in the other room while
important men in dark suits were eating their dinner.
Stalin was there. The shot rang out. It was Her, Nadja.
Stalin runs out of the room.

In reality, Nadja was by herself. They told him later, at
a dinner with his boys. Stalin was in shock. He thought
of himself as a "sincere intellectual," in charge of the
New World Order.

Stalin   Yes, let's publish and promote the poet, Mayakovsky,
                he was a man of the People.
                He said, later on, when the poet was long dead.
Stalin   He was a damned good poet. The real deal.
Kirov   (We were *bona fide* Communists, in those days, the
                days of Mayakovsky, planning a new and better world.)
                Stalin ran out of the room.
                His wife, Nadja, was on the floor.
                What had she been thinking?

Nadja	I can't stand it anymore. It's a joke. These people are creeps.
	A shot. They look up.
	Stalin runs out of the room.
	There she is on the floor. Blood pouring out of her mouth.
Masha	(It wasn't like that. She'd shot herself in the heart. She was in bed at the time, in her mirrored room. Lace covered the furniture. Her gun was underneath a maroon pillow, embroidered with the Communist emblem, the hammer and sickle. She lay down, thought awhile, then shot herself with the little Mauser.)
	What happens in the man Stalin's fucking brain?
	We will never know.
	A shot. The guests look up. Stalin runs out of the room.
	Nobody says anything.
	Maybe there was a doctor, but Nadja was dead on the floor in the hall.
Masha	(No doctor. They found her later. On her bed. Stalin couldn't speak. Shot with a Mauser, Communist style.)
	Back in the '20s, my father was running up and down stairs. In Brooklyn tenements. Russia had become the Soviet Union.
Masha	("She has a big hole in her heart," the doctor said, when he was finally summoned. Stalin hid out for days and days. The functionaries stayed in their dachas.)
Nadja	(Can you believe it? What goes on?)
	They liked Mausers for their dirty business, these people.

Scene 2

Volodya shacked up with a married couple. Lily and Osip Brik. They both loved him, apparently.
It was Lily, later on during the Soviet empire, who begged Stalin to restore Mayakovsky's reputation as a Revolutionary Poet.
Stalin, who had nothing to lose, responded immediately:

Stalin   Mayakovsky was and remains the best, most gifted poet of our Soviet epoch. Indifference to his memory and his work is a crime. Kirov?

Kirov   No two ways about it, Comrade.

Lily somehow had that connection to Stalin. Someone who knew someone. She had herself once been a known commodity of stage and screen along with her sister Elsa, a writer.
In the old days, they had procured the young Cossack poet as one of their own, a true ménage-à-trois of the new world, where one was free to love.

Osip   So what do you do for a living?

Mayakovsky   I'm a poet.

Lily   Can you live?

Mayakovsky   In the new world, everything will be different. Even poets will live, because they, too, are hard workers and sincere intellectuals.

Lily   What else do you do?

Mayakovsky   I gamble.

Osip   You can live on that?

Mayakovsky   I live.

Mazel tov.

Mayakovsky	We live in a new world. Love is free now. The married can fuck the stranger, the old can fuck the young, and so on.
Lily	Do we do it together?
Osip	I don't know about that.
Lily	Volodya?
Mayakovsky	For you, I would do it.
Osip	Not so fast.
Lily	I love you both. But I'm still free. I do what I want.
Osip	Maybe once. *(Pause)* I don't think so.
Lily	Let's see what happens.
Osip	I don't think so.

It was a lot like the sixties.

"I don't share my women." I actually remember saying that. Years ago. Seems so foolish now.

It's a new era. They were the hipsters of their day. They looked and sounded just like us. Great costumes. Movies were a brand new radical art form.

My father started hanging out at the Brooklyn Paramount around 1929. Learning how to run the picture show.

But man is the same as he always was, only there's more of us, too many of us.

Homo Sapiens.

We love our poetry and our art. Our theater and movies.

Whales don't go to the movies. Wolves don't go to the movies. Only we go to the movies.

But man is the same. Big forces control his Fate. His life is easily ruined. By bad luck, passion, addiction and so on . . .

Scene 3

Osip	What do you play, Volodya?
Lily	By the way.
Osip	What do you play?
Mayakovsky	Whatever I can.
Lily	You don't say?
Mayakovsky	Whenever I can. I love it. Hey, rhyming is what I play, Osip, Rhyming! It's just like gambling, a throw of the dice!
Osip	No, it isn't.
Lily	What about Love? We can love, not only ourselves. Not only ourselves. Like elephants and wolves.
Mayakovsky	But it's difficult. Difficult. We don't like sacrifice. Though sometimes we must. People rushing about.
Lily	What do you mean?
Mayakovsky	People rushing about. In search of meaning, food, money, love, freedom. Comfort.
Lily	Comfort.
Osip	Some people must be wrong about that. I think some people are wrong about that.
Mayakovsky	Not to doubt is important.
Lily	You think so?
Mayakovsky	I do.
Osip	I don't know.
Mayakovsky	We must be able to act, to live freely. We must behave as if we're eating together, feeling together.
Lily	And time is passing.

Osip	We do the best we can.
Mayakovsky	Unless we stop.
Osip	What's that?
Mayakovsky	We stop.
Lily	Stop?
Mayakovsky	Stop. *(Pause, screams.)* STOP! *(Pause)*
Lily	And then?
Mayakovsky	Things go on. Things always go on. *(Pause)* They don't stop. But now we must have faith in the coming Revolution.

Scene 4

Lily	I don't like the guy.
Oslp	He talks too much.
Lily	His teeth are bad.
Osip	He's too tall.
Lily	He writes weird.
Osip	I like his stuff.
Lily	I don't.
Osip	And he's broke.
Lily	He gambles.
Osip	Don't loan him money.
Lily	No worries, darling.
Osip	Dearest.
Lily	They call him the "love boat."
Osip	He floats around. Reads his poems. Talks to the girls.
Lily	I think he's insecure. He's a Cossack. Terrible teeth and he talks too much and his poems suck.

18

Scene 5

Elsa	What's wrong with Mayakovsky?
Lily	Terrible teeth and he talks too much and his poems suck.
Elsa	He seems nice.
Lily	He's tall. Very intelligent. He's a poet. And he writes plays.
Elsa	I've done one of them. Maybe more than one.
Lily	Can you say a line?
Elsa	Yes.
Lily	Say it.
Elsa	"My verses will reach you over the mountains of centuries." How's that?
Lily	Not great, I don't think.
Elsa	Very poetic.
Lily	Plays in verses. Not good.
Elsa	Osip?
Lily	My husband loves him, so maybe I'll love him, too. He's hungry for love, and so am I. We need to be loved by each other. We weren't meant to be alone. It's the human species. And we act.
Elsa	We are actors.
Lily	(I don't know about you, dear. You're not there quite yet.)
Elsa	It's fun. It's what we do. I love it.
Lily	There's lots of attention there.
Elsa	Exactly.
Lily	But that's not all. It's another level of reality.

Elsa	I like that.
Lily	Another dimension.
Elsa	Definitely.
Lily	Sex is definitely involved. Sex is involved with everything.
Elsa	Sex and killing. And power. You're slight but strong.
Lily	I know.
Elsa	And pretty.
Lily	I know.
Elsa	A classic Russian.
	They are Jewesses. Mercantile. From Moscow.
Lily	It's true. Look, there he is.
	Enter Mayakovsky.
Elsa	He's tall.
Lily	Look at those teeth.
Elsa	Brutish.
Lily	Look at that face.
Elsa	Slavic.
Lily	Look at his clothes.
Elsa	Tattered.
Lily	He can't stop talking.
Elsa	Rubbish.
Mayakovsky	(Look. She's part of my family now. The little pretty one.) I don't know how she did that. She made a little family out of us.
	Says Mayakovsky.
	(She's a Jew.)
	And so is her husband, Osip.
	He's a Jew, too.
Lily	He looks intimidated. The poet.

Elsa	He couldn't fuck a dove.
Lily	I know.
Elsa	I don't know what I mean by that.
Lily	I don't either.
Mayakovsky	(She really turned me on, and she knew it, and she used it. She liked power.)
	Soso.
Mayakovsky	(I wanted her so badly, I was so in love, as they say, that I came too soon.)
	Soso. Was Stalin's nickname as a boy.
Lily	I like action in a man.
Mayakovsky	(She was not that sincere as an intellectual, but she was open, and interesting, and promiscuous. She knew some things. Lily. About men.)
Osip	She treated Mayakovsky like a big dog. You could say.
Lily	And then, later on, he falls in love with a younger woman, Tatyana, a Parisienne, so he blows his heart out.
	Just Like Nadja, years ago, but nothing like Nadja.
Lily	So they say. But they don't really know.
Osip	Somebody heard two shots. Maybe it was the Communists, after all.
Lily	He had a lot of problems with the bureaucrats.
Osip	Mayakovsky?
Lily	Yes. Wouldn't you?
Osip	I don't know what to say.
Lily	On the other hand, he had a good time traveling and going to spas. Readings. Two or three a day. The students started shouting at him.
Mayakovsky	He's a narcissist!, *they shouted.*
	Comrade Narcissist!

Mayakovsky	(Can you beat that?)
	He tried to tell them to sit down.
Mayakovsky	Sit down and shut up! You ignorant shits!
	He lost his voice.
Lily	No time to complain about the revolution, though the authorities didn't bother him much. Toward the end he was having problems. He kept talking about killing himself, and then he did it.
Osip	She wouldn't come to him—Tatyana. She wouldn't fuck him, so he blew his heart away. That's how I see it.
	Who was that?
Lily	An actress, I forget her name now, it will come to me, hang on, she lived in Paris, I think, and she didn't want to come to Russia, something like that, and join him there.
	But that's not a reason, that's not a good enough reason.
Lily	Tatyana was her name. He always wanted to, that's what I'm saying. Kill himself. I think he was pretty neurotic and fucked up and too much in love.
	Yes. I can remember her name now. Tatyana. Sorry.
Osip	(He had suicide in mind. All along. That's what he was thinking about.)
	What were they all thinking? About murder and suicide and exile? Can you imagine?
	Why he had suicide in mind, he and Nadja, what were they thinking, back in the old days, the days of the Russian Revolution and the Soviet Union.
	We may never know.

	She's lying on the bed. No one's around. Her husband
	thinks he's a sincere intellectual, doing what he's
	supposed to do, and so on, so there's a problem there.
	With his thinking.
Nadja	Yes.
	And she—
Nadja	This is all creepy. Things are not right, and sex is dirty.
	What? Say again?
Nadja	I said, sex is dirty.
Lily	No, it's not. It's the biological imperative. That's how babies are born. And being in love is the most exciting thing of all. For a human being.
	Doused by tribalism and Group Thought. Fettered by anxiety and custom. Think of Freud and what he came to in his writings. Think of the survival of the gene pool.
Lily	I was thinking of Mayakovsky and his complicated love life, and my own.
	I was thinking of what Nadja is thinking.
Nadja	How I'm not loved.
	How they shot themselves in the heart.
	Why Lily was so interesting.
Lily	The reproductive process be damned. Fidelity be damned.
	Believing everything they did was right.
	Though I'm not so sure about Mayakovsky. I think his mind was addled, with too much of this and too much of that, he was a germ freak, and he was too tall by a long shot.
	What would they say now?

Kirov	(Stalin is a man of delusion. He will kill for what he believes in. Meanwhile, he is a slave to everyone around him, and everyone around him is his slave.)
Mayakovsky	(I love her, and at the same time I see that it's an illusion, or maybe not; definitely, I feel something, or I'm in awe, or fascinated, infatuated, but I feel the heartache, and at the same time, I don't know, I don't know what will happen, I don't know what she'll do, I don't know.)

Scene 6

Lily	His mind was not clear, if that has anything to do with it.
Elsa	Let's read one of his poems.
	A short one.
Elsa	Sounds good.
	Let's go.
Mayakovsky	Don't waste your rays, sun! Glare!
	Let thousands of my disciples be born
	to trumpet anathemas on the squares!
	And when at last there comes,
	stepping onto the peaks of the ages,
	chillingly,
	the last of their days,
	in the black souls of anarchists and killers
	I, a gory vision, will blaze!
	That's enough. Way enough.
	I couldn't agree more. *(Of himself)* Sounds to me like he was out of his mind.

Volodya, the Anti-Christ.

The poem is called All *and* Everything. *Go figure. This is one year before the Bolshevik Revolution. I mean the poem. Was written. You can see them now in the Moscow apartment:*

Lily   What's happening, Volodya?

Mayakovsky   People are rioting in the streets. Milling about. Men are coming home without legs, without arms, with bloody, bandaged heads.

Lily   What can we do?

Mayakovsky   We must stay out of it.

Lily   How can we stay out of it?

Mayakovsky   Just stay out of it.

Lily   No. I want to do plays. I want to do film.

Mayakovsky   So do I.

Lily   So we can't stay out of it. We're only human. We must participate. Do what we do.

Mayakovsky   Osip is worried about these Communists. I don't know if I like their thinking. They want to organize the State, Lily. They want to organize power. He thinks they want to make us like automatons. Like ants. I don't like it, either. It's not the kind of future I'm interested in. But it is a future. Something new. And it's true about the class struggle.

Lily   We're not working class or middle class or any class. We're artists, Volodya.

Mayakovsky   Exactly. But I get up every day and I work, I try to work, I work, I want to participate in living, having a purpose, a life, a literary life.
(To himself) The Russians, they had talent.

Lily

(To Chorus) This comes as a surprise to you?
They were just like us. I'm thinking of Nadja, whatever
her last name was. Alliluyeva. Stalin. Alone in her
room. Mirrors and white lace. Despised those guys.
Dark suits and high boots. Hanging around. Running
the State. Apparatus. Alone in her room. Wondering
what. She was. Thinking about. Blowing her heart
away with the Mauser. Two kids.
The Sincere Intellectual.
An Unknown woman vanished by the State. A tiny
little wheel in the apparatus. A womb in the apparatus.
Nadja. Disappeared.

Nadja

I'm going now. I've had enough. Go fuck yourself. Go
kill yourself. You and all your buddies bud-bud too, go
fuck yourselves. In the ear. With your lies and your
dreams and your murderous fantasies, go away and die
in a pit, in an earthen pit, which is where you will all
end; you'll end up there, anyway, no matter what you
do, that's where you will end, my friend, in a cold and
empty pit in the earth, a filthy piece of organic matter
in the earth. This is what I think of you, Pal.
She said. To herself.

Scene 7

Speaks the Young Sincere Intellectual to his cronies. He
was called Koba in those early days.

Stalin

All right. Sacrifice. Let's talk about that. Sacrifices have
to be made. If you need money, I will give you money.
If you need help, I will give you help. If you need time,

	I will give you time. But you must stay on the path. That's all I ask.
Kirov	What is the path, Comrade?
Stalin	What the fuck are you talking about, Kirov? Marxist-Leninism. Idiot!
Kirov	That's what I meant, sir.
Stalin	There, you have it. You have it right there. With your comrades, to make a historical truth. A reality. Without God or religion or the supernatural. Without guidance from the well-born, the rich, or the filthy politicians.
Kirov	Religion is deep in this country, Koba.
Stalin	We must unearth it, Kirov.
Kirov	The customs of our people are also deep.
Stalin	We must uproot them. But there must be leaders. There must be accountability. We can't have people running around giving orders to other people.
Kirov	I agree.
Stalin	Let's hear what we must do from those above us.
Kirov	They are workers like us, revolutionaries, like us.
Stalin	Without hierarchy is chaos. Everyone thinks they're important. Everyone thinks they should be immortal. Everyone has a life to protect, a family to protect, his pleasures and his hobbies, his beliefs and his occupations. Everyone thinks he's right.
Kirov	No one thinks he's wrong.
Stalin	But inferiors. They'll be wiped out. The forces of the Revolution will wipe them out. Those that think they are inferior and those that are. The entire bourgeoisie. The artists and poets. The Christians and Jews. Our

	leaders will emerge from the struggle. That is how true
	leaders emerge, from the struggle for life.
Kirov	Yes, this must be so.
Stalin	It can be no other way, Comrade.

Scene 8

Years later, Lily wrote a letter to Stalin, asking Him to save the career of Volodya Mayakovsky. The name itself sounds like a poem.
Volodya Mayakovsky.

Lily   "Dear Stalin, you alone can make a resurrection—
The important avant-garde poetry of my dear, lost
friend Vladimir Mayakovsky, who killed himself in
despair at thirty-six years of age. He was a very
important Russian Revolutionary poet from the
Caucasus, like you, a big, tall man, a founder of the
Futurist movement, a Cossack, a Communist, maybe he
became disillusioned, I don't know about that, an
important poet of the Revolution, so you should restore
him, Dear Leader, to his rightful place in the cultural
history of the Soviet Union. Yours truly, Lilyana Brik."
Lily.
A draft to the Sincere Intellectual.
*Stalin thought about it. Mayakovsky was restored to
historical existence. Stalin had nothing to lose. An
abstract fucked-up poet who killed himself and did no
harm to the Party. A Futurist without a future.*
Nadja was never spoken of, they say, even to his kids.

*I don't know how they know all this. So much is
disappeared—the Provençal poets, the Greeks—the
Futurists—the "modern" attitude, free love and free
expression, without mobile phones and the internet,
and whatever gadgets are still to come, in the pipeline,
as they say, coming down the tube, for killing and
virtual brains and instant art and orgasms with robots,
and drones, and so on—they were the avant-garde of
life, in those days, Lily and Osip and Volodya.
Turns out Lily and Osip were Jews. Go figure.*

Lily   There was a boy I liked in school. I had an abortion
when I was seventeen. My parents loved me. They never
pushed religion on me. We went places. The society is
changing and I'm changed. I'm an actress. I think that's
the biggest revolution of all, in these revolutionary
times, the revolution in the mind, where one can
become a role, reach another dimension—*(To Osip)*
Excuse me?

Osip   Slow down, Lilyana.

Lily   No. I just don't believe in any of that horseshit.

Osip   Neither do I.

Lily   The Revolution is here.

Mayakovsky   The Revolution is still coming.

Osip   It's on its way.

Lily   It's here already.

Osip   It will turn us into automatons.

Mayakovsky   We are already automatons. We've lost the war in the
West. Lenin is our only hope now. We must wish them
all well.

Lily	Take care of your teeth, Volodya. And take that cigarette out of your mouth. And stop trying to screw every girl you lay eyes on. And stop gambling on everything that could possibly happen next.
Mayakovsky	And you?
Lily	Me, what?
Mayakovsky	What'll you do?
Lily	I'll be on stage, I'll be in the cinema.
Mayakovsky	What'll you give up for the Revolution?
Lily	Fidelity. I don't know what I mean by that. *She doesn't, really.*
Mayakovsky	You must give up something.
Lily	You don't know anything about it.
Mayakovsky	It's called sacrifice.
Lily	You're teasing me, Volodya.
Osip	It's called Revolution. How long will it take, Volodya, for the Revolution to start to stink?
Mayakovsky	When they start killing each other. Cinema, eh, Lily?
Lily	Yes, Volodya.
Mayakovsky	You're spoiled, Lily, by your looks.
Lily	I don't care. I have talent. I want to do what I want. To do.
Osip	The beginning and end of the Revolution—
Lily	When I want and with whom I want.
Osip	—Is here. The end of the end. The beginning is the end.
Mayakovsky	Wordplay, Osip.
Osip	Yes. I agree. That's what I do. Gambling is a sickness, Volodya, because you always lose.
Mayakovsky	We are what we are.
Lily	And you hate to lose.

Mayakovsky	And you? You don't know what you are. You say you do, but you don't.
Lily	But I do.
Mayakovsky	How so?
Lily	Through Art and Revolution.
Mayakovsky	You don't know.
Lily	I do know.
Mayakovsky	Art and Revolution. *(Pause)* (I feel like these ignoramuses are giving me a hard time. They don't know any better. They're trying to survive, like any brutish animal. It's my own fault. But I have actual talent, a gift from the gods. Talent, and intelligence, and good looks, and I'm tall, too! Bad teeth is a problem, true, and the womanizing, and throwing money away on games of chance.)
Lily	You drink too much, Volodya.

He starts to say something sarcastic, but thinks better of it. He lights a cigarette and looks at the sky. Lights of Moscow. No stars. Noise of drunks brawling in the streets. Lily looks at his tobacco-stained mouth.

Scene 9

Stalin is sitting with a crony. Around a fire in the woods. He liked that kind of thing. Camping, fishing.

Stalin	So the old slut writes me a letter about her former boyfriend, the poet, Mayakovsky. You remember him?
Kirov	No.
Stalin	Lilyana Brik. You know her?
Kirov	No.

Stalin	This was in the old days, before we took over the State.
Kirov	Before my time.
Stalin	Yes. You were in knickers.
Kirov	So I never met her.
Stalin	Jewish couple. The Briks. They took him in. Lousy poet. Never wrote about anything real, anything useful. Mayakovsky.
Kirov	He killed himself when he was young? Yes?
Stalin	Yes. 36. We won't talk about that.
Kirov	No.
Stalin	It's too depressing.
Kirov	Of course. Bad poetry is depressing.
Stalin	I had a dream last night. It had no meaning, like this fellow's poetry. *(Pause)* *Stalin looks expectantly at Kirov.*
Kirov	What was the dream, Comrade?
Stalin	All right, I'll tell you. It wasn't much.
Kirov	Please.
Stalin	Good people were coming and going. Good men, so I was happy. They were dressed in yellow. That's all I remember.
Kirov	Yellow?
Stalin	Yes, the good men were dressed in yellow. I was happy to see them. I woke up feeling happy to have seen them. *(Pause)* What do you make of that?
Kirov	I don't know what to make of it.
Stalin	No, not much there.
Kirov	No.
Stalin	Various good men in yellow. Coming and going. *(Pause)* He was not a good poet, this Mayakovsky.

	From the Caucasus. But in the West they don't know
	what's good or bad. He has a modern reputation.
	Modern, up to date. She wants me to rehabilitate him.
Kirov	Why?
Stalin	You know how that is. It would give her own life meaning.
Kirov	I see. Meaning. A lover?
Stalin	Yes. They had abandoned the Socialist project. Self-important hedonist aesthetes.
Kirov	What can you expect from the Jews?
Stalin	He was a Cossack, Mayakovsky, from the Caucasus, like me. Not a Jew, like so many of these fellows.
Kirov	Yes. I knew that, Comrade.
Stalin	Probably he went to a religious school. When he was young. Artistic. Design. A ferocious gambler. That's well known. And he read his poetry all over the country. It was a big deal in those days.
Kirov	Many in the party are Jewish.
Stalin	Yes, Kirov, but not this poet. Mayakovsky. A Cossack. From the Caucasus, like me. *(Pause)* Yes, one day I'll clean it up, make it straight with History.

What did he mean by that?

Stalin	The Briks and her husband—I forget his name— Osip—they were business people. Jews. His family was in coral. Siberia. What her parents were doing, I can't remember. But they did well. They went to spas. They traveled.
Kirov	Elite bourgeoisie. No more of that.
Stalin	No. *(Pause)* Ah. This is what I like, Kirov. A bit of nature. Living rough. A fire.

He had like fifty servants and sycophants with him.
Or psychopaths. On his little jaunts to the sea and
the woods.

Kirov   What will you do? About the poet.

Stalin   Between you and me, it's a gesture to the West. I'll
approve him, publish him, avoid punishing his girlfriends.
Glamorize his suicide, his modernity. Between you and
me, he was a lousy poet, self-indulgent, self-pitying, not a
practical, socialist man. But we'll say he was with us in his
ideology. We make History, Comrade, so we must have
strict standards. Yes. In industry, in agriculture, in the
arts. All and everywhere. I'll clean it all up, eventually.
You are a Jew, are you not, Kirov?

Kirov   No. Russian Orthodox. Now I am a Bolshevik,
a Marxist.

Stalin   Yes, you said that. Of course. That fellow over there,
you see him? He was looking at me. He, too, is Jewish.

Kirov   Half-Jewish.

Stalin   He was looking at me, that asshole.

Kirov   I didn't notice.

Stalin   Don't look.

Kirov   I'm not looking.

Stalin   Asshole.

Kirov   He looks at people. That's what he does.

Stalin   Asshole.

Kirov   He looks kindly, protectively.

Stalin   He's trying to catch my gaze, my glance, but he won't
catch it.

Kirov   He's ambitious.

Stalin   That's certain, but he won't catch my eye.

Kirov	He means well.
Stalin	Everyone means well, Kirov.
Kirov	True.
Stalin	We're still building here. We're building. And then, we'll see. Is he still watching me?
Kirov	No. He's holding forth to the comrades now. He's highly thought of. He rises in the Party.
Stalin	Yes, his day will come. I gave him money years ago, you know—I can't remember his name—in the oil fields of Baku. Not a loan. I just gave out money in those days. For the Party. No questions asked.
Kirov	You still do, Comrade.
Stalin	The Party is like a pyramid, Kirov. I learned this when I was in school, in Tiflis. A pyramid. Many squares. A broad bottom, and on the top—one square. Only One.
Kirov	But there's movement amongst the squares.
Stalin	Of course. There's attrition, sickness and death. Betrayal, confusion, and so on. But at the top there must be one, one single voice, so that the Party can function and reach its Destiny. Do you follow me?
Kirov	I think so, Comrade.
Stalin	Just the same, there's no contradiction there. It's all there in the Bible. Along with Marx and Lenin, of course.
Kirov	And Trotsky?
Stalin	Trotsky is finished. Don't talk to me about Trotsky. *The Sincere Intellectual attended seminary in his youth. As a teen-ager, he gave it up in favor of Marxism—party brigandage and revolutionary organizing.*

Stalin	Words, *he says.* Now we are actually doing it. Living History, Kirov.

Scene 10

Years before, Elsa is speaking with her brother-in-law.

Elsa	What's wrong with you, Osip?
Osip	I beg your pardon?
Elsa	There's something wrong with your thinking. Do you mind?
Osip	Not at all, Elsa.
Elsa	You let your wife do whatever she wants, with whomever she wants. She acts like a slut and she drinks and who knows what else? And now you go around like a trio, her and you and Mayakovsky. And they carry on, and you do nothing. What's wrong with your thinking?
Osip	A person doesn't own another person. People are weak and they have desires. What attitude is one to take? There are too many rules, too many strictures. If I love a person, it is my loyalty that counts. I am steadfast. It has nothing to do with romance. Romance has nothing to do with it. Sex has nothing to do with it. There is not enough love in the world. I have committed myself to the revolution of society and its ways, and there I will remain—true to my wife till the end of our days.
Elsa	But what happens when mistakes are made, Osip?
Osip	Ah, mistakes.
Elsa	Mistakes.

Osip	Why does a young man, like me, Elsa, leave his home for a girl?
Elsa	I don't know, I'm sure.
Osip	So. He leaves to get laid, and leaves to get laid, and then he is left himself, by himself, like a dog? Like a cringing dog? What was he thinking? Wanting to be loyal with his wife and yet risking her love? Losing loyalty and self-respect. Losing honor in the name of sex, and then his bags are in the hall, the locks are changed, and she's moved to San Francisco or Bad Mannheim or someplace? What about that? Or you tell your mistress you will never marry her, even though she's the only one who loves you truly? Or, better yet, she has an abortion—the only child you'll ever have? And so on.
Elsa	Did that happen to you?
Osip	No. These are only examples. Mistakes.
	I think he's lying.
Elsa	Lily did that, at seventeen, Osip—I brought her out of town, to a certain spa. The father was a certain Harry Blumenfeld.
Osip	I'm telling you, Elsa, there's only remorse—the ones you left, the ones who left you. The reasons are gone, the impulses are lost. You can't remember their faces. And you wonder what were you doing at the time. I'm telling you, Elsa. You never get over these things. Permanent scars are made.
Elsa	What about you and Lily and Volodya Mayakovsky?
Osip	Between me and Lily, it's sacred. We'll never part, until death. Mayakovsky is a friend, and he won't last.

Elsa	What do you mean, "he won't last."
Osip	He won't last. That's all.

Scene 11

Who was Harry Blumenfeld? Someone just like us. Not knowing what he was doing, not knowing what to do, nor why, while time passes and death looms and now oblivion, soon enough.
C'est la vie.
Hurting people and being hurt for no reason. I imagine Lily now, a pretty young woman, a fallen woman, living the new life, a secular revolutionary, as she travels with her sister, Elsa:

Lily	We are going abroad together, dear. We're taking the baths. Aren't you glad?
Elsa	We're not taking the baths. We're having a procedure. Remember, you pay the doctor, the spa, and tip everybody.
Lily	I wish Mom would have come.
Elsa	She's had enough. I can handle it.
	I know her mind. There are rules. There are laws and society. You're not married, and the father is a fool. And you're too young. *(Pause)* It's because life is precious. Because on the other side is death. Because if life exists, then God exists. And life exists. We are here. We must live well and praise God. In the synagogue, we rise and praise, rise and praise. We are Jews, and we have laws.
Lily	That's Mom, not you. I don't go to synagogue. And neither do you.

Elsa	From now on, maybe we'll both go.
Lily	No. We don't live like Jews. We live like *them*, the Gentiles.
Lily	These are the times we live in.
Elsa	Things change, but people stay the same. That's what I think.
Lily	No, they don't.
Elsa	People are always the same. They are never different. No matter what people say or do, they are always the same.
Lily	I don't know what you're talking about.
Elsa	No, you don't.
Lily	I really don't know what you're talking about.
Elsa	(I'll tell you: Two blood-shot eyes and a wide, dumb Cossack head. Two dirty feet, two hairy arms. Killing for food. Killing for comfort. For a big name. For power. For sex. For drink. Easter time: A pogrom. Kill the Jews and take their money. Nothing's changed.) These people, these politicians, these artsy friends of yours, these contemporaries—they are deluded. Bad things will happen. It is opening up before us like a maw. Like a hurricane. People with new ideas, but nothing will change. It's nothing new and nothing will change. It's a law of nature. We are a species that never learns.
Lily	You read too many books.
Elsa	I don't read enough.
Lily	I don't agree with you.
Elsa	Who cares?
Lily	Think of science, Elsa.

Elsa	No, you think of it—outside there is change, yes, as we go around ruining everything. Ruining nature, ruining life. Wasting our lives.
Lily	We are saving lives, improving lives.
Elsa	There's too much of it. Too much life.
Lily	How can you say that? Who goes to synagogue and bows to life?
Elsa	Not to life, to God. They are not the same. I've contradicted myself. That's all right. That's my opinion.
Lily	You've contradicted yourself.
Elsa	I don't care.
Lily	We don't bow anymore. We don't believe anymore.
Elsa	That's why the world will come crushing down on our stupid little heads. Before we can do anything worthwhile.
Lily	I don't think so. I think a new world is coming. Soon. Actually, it's here.
Elsa	We've lost our heritage. We've forgotten how to bow. The new world will kick us as it comes. Mark my words. *(Pause)*
Lily	It's not fair, Elsa.
Elsa	Life's not fair, Lily, as I'm sure you've heard already from your stupid, Futurist friends. I think I'll be a writer when I get old enough and wise enough.
Lily	Did you say, "writer?"
Elsa	Yes, why not?
Lily	You're too silly to know anything.
Elsa	Look who's talking.
Lily	I want freedom, Elsa. I wish to be free. I want to act and play roles and think the way I think and talk the

	way I talk, and be with whom I want to be and be an actress and aim high, to another dimension even, and yes, be famous.
	Actually, Elsa became somewhat famous in her day, writing in French.
Elsa	And remember, tip everyone who helps you, don't talk too much, and don't flirt.
	Spas. I was working as a busboy in the Catskills, a long time ago. A Kuchalein. Basically, a run-down house off a dirt road in the woods. The guests were Holocaust survivors, mostly Germans. They never spoke, they stayed silent, except for complaining about the food. There was one old man who'd been a doctor in the Soviet Union before the Purge. He liked to tell stories about the Siberian gulags.
	It was a hard job. I was only fourteen years old, but I've been interested in Stalin ever since.
	Years later, when he had been established in power:

Scene 12

Stalin	Morons.
Voroshilov	Sir?
Stalin	Nothing.
	Stalin and his closest cronies have gone hunting. With him is a favorite crony called Voroshilov. They all like hunting.
Stalin	This is fun. This is it. Out in the fresh air. No papers to sign. Nobody you have to convince, one way or another. This is it. What was I saying?

Voroshilov	Something about morons.
Stalin	Of course. Morons. But we must keep them in a straight line, just like the geese, eh, who make a perfect "V" and who fly perfectly together. You see? Yes! We must keep to our aim. But it's good to get out in the country Yes! Kill the birds. Kill the animals. Overhear each other.
Voroshilov	Sir?
Stalin	Keep an eye on each other.
Voroshilov	Shoot the breeze.
Stalin	Smell the air.
Voroshilov	Take a shit in the grass.
Stalin	Smell the grass.
Voroshilov	Get some exercise.
Stalin	Right you are. And take a piss wherever you want.
Voroshilov	Build a fire. Set up a tent. Cook a fresh meal, freshly killed.
Stalin	Build a fire.
Voroshilov	I said that.
Stalin	Take a break from monotonous thinking.
Voroshilov	Sir?
Stalin	Take a break.
Voroshilov	I am, Comrade. Taking a break. Enjoying it thoroughly.
Stalin	Good.
Voroshilov	I love it.
Stalin	Unlike the morons in the West, who have it upside down, who think life is free, who want to have a good time, who like property, democracy, competition, and all that.
Voroshilov	I totally agree.

Stalin	Because we're always right, you know, our ideology is impeccable. Historical science, or the science of history, call it whatever you want.
Voroshilov	Only a moron could not understand what we're doing, or trying to do, sir.
Stalin	Exactly. Trying. Fighting.
Voroshilov	Constantly.
Stalin	But it's good to get away from the weight, the weight of determined history, in which we, we are the actors, we are the agency of this Determination, it is we who decide.
Voroshilov	I like that.
Stalin	We are the agents of a Just Cause. We are the actors. Yes, and we must rehearse our lines, and cast the parts, and prepare for action on the stage. We must aim and not miss, for History has no qualms.
Voroshilov	Good analogy.
Stalin	History has no mercy. And so we must pay, because no one has a free ticket to the show, Comrade Voroshilov, we must pay for the privilege, being both the witness and the actor, for the result.
Voroshilov	I didn't follow you there, Sir.
Stalin	No, you didn't. But that's all right. So long as I heard it for myself. We've made a lot of mistakes, but we have learned our lessons well. Yes, soon we will do some shooting.
Voroshilov	Almost there, Sir.
Stalin	Ready, aim, fire!
Voroshilov	Kaboom! *(Laughter, sound of an explosion, off.)*

This was before Nadja blew her heart away with the
Mauser. There was Stalin's first wife—Ekaterina—
what ever happened to her?
She died. Long ago. In the Caucasus. True to her man.
Here is Nadja, in her room:

Scene 13

Nadja	I don't understand. What would happen if I left a note? What would I say? That I'm not history, that I'm not anything, that I'm not? I don't exist, as it is. I am a fountain, maybe, a bloodstream. Not even that. A heartbeat. A breath. Call the doctor. Get an opinion. Find out what's what. What the fuck is going on? *(Enter Masha)*
Masha	Madame?
Nadja	What do you want, Masha?
Masha	Nothing. You called?
Nadja	No, I didn't, but since you're here, you can answer some questions.
Masha	I have no answers, Madam.
Nadja	It doesn't matter. Just make them up. The first one is this: What is the meaning of life? *(Pause)* Say something.
Masha	To love your neighbor and fear God?
Nadja	No. That is not an answer.
Masha	I have no answers, then.
Nadja	I know you do have answers, Masha. The world is being destroyed in front of our eyes. Why?

Masha	Because sin and iniquity rule the world. So it will be destroyed, as in the time of Sodom and Gomorrah.
Nadja	Why?
Masha	Because of the wickedness of our rulers.
Nadja	Ah.
Masha	People hate their neighbors and ignore God, or don't know God, or don't fear God, or have no understanding of God.
Nadja	Like me. And you? How do you understand God?
Masha	I don't, Madam. I'm the same as you.
Nadja	No, you're not. Come on, Masha. Come up with something. Speak!
Masha	God is the Spirit of the Universe?
Nadja	No. God can't be God and the universe. It would mean that everything is God. So what's the point of praying to everything? You see what I mean?
Masha	No.
Nadja	What about Jesus?
Masha	He gave his life for the Gentiles, Madam.
Nadja	Why?
Masha	Because they say it was ordained in their bible.
Nadja	Who says so?
Masha	The Gentiles said so. It's in their bible. The Messiah will come in the End Times, to forgive the sins of the people. And the wicked will go to Hell.
Nadja	What did we do wrong, Masha?
Masha	We are impure.
Nadja	That's for sure. We eat, shit and fornicate. Sorry, Masha. I know you don't like to hear that kind of talk.

	We'll start over. *(Pause)* To save us from Hell, Masha.
	Where is Hell?
Masha	Where?
Nadja	Let's say it's here, Masha. This is Hell. And He was
	tortured in the flesh, He suffered in His material flesh, to
	show us the meaning of life, which is nothing, Masha.
	Which is suffering, Masha. And His life goes back to the
	Father. So who is the Father? Is He a man, like a *kulak*
	with a beard? Is he Jewish? Never mind. Jesus Christ
	suffered, and He gave His suffering for us. So that we
	might be forgiven. So that we might be purified. He
	suffered for our sins. I like that idea. And he was a Jew.
	It's all very confusing, Masha. And that's why we got
	rid of it. Not we, them. Not them, Lenin and his friends.
	They got rid of the Christian religion. We had a revolution
	here, Masha. Now we have History and the State, in the
	hands of my husband, the Sincere Intellectual. No more
	heaven, no more hell. Just this. You follow me?
Masha	I think so.
Nadja	Good.
Masha	Are you all right, Madam?
Nadja	No.
Masha	I'm sorry.
Nadja	So am I. Whatever happened to that first wife?
	Ekaterina? No one will say what happened to her.
Masha	She died of something.
Nadja	What? What did she die of?
Masha	I don't know, Ma'am. She was still young. Typhoid,
	maybe.
Nadja	Leave me alone now. Please.

Scene 14

Lily storms out of the ménage à trois, irritated by reality.

Lily   Whatever reality is, I don't care. Life as we know it is over. I just want to live. Whatever reality is, I don't care. *(Lily exits)*

Mayakovsky   Why do you let her do as she pleases?

Osip   I don't own her.

Mayakovsky   You took marriage vows, Osya.

Osip   Very secular. A civic commitment. A civilized commitment between civilized people who understand society and its ways.

Mayakovsky   These ways have evolved over thousands of years.

Osip   Causing misery and conflict.

Mayakovsky   And families.

Osip   And more and more people, blotting out nature. What good is it to have so many people?

Mayakovsky   It's nature's way.

Osip   Then the hell with nature, Volodya. It has to stop.

Mayakovsky   That's the whole idea of the revolution, is it not? To control nature? To harness and direct economic forces?

Osip   Do you think it's working? Tell me honestly.

Mayakovsky   I don't know. I hope for the best.

Osip   War is happening. Killing is happening. Will you go to war?

Mayakovsky   No. Will you?

Osip   No.

Mayakovsky   They lit a fire and now it's burning out of control.

Osip	It would be stupid to die that way.
Mayakovsky	They've built the coffins for the boys who aren't killed yet. They've got truckloads of crutches, prosthetic arms and legs. It's disgusting.
Osip	What will you do?
Mayakovsky	I'll go and hide out somewhere.
Osip	They'll take the Jews first. Always. Fodder for the cannons. We'll run.
Mayakovsky	You haven't answered my question. About Lily.
Osip	I can't control her any more than I can control the war, Volodya. And neither can you. I can hardly control myself. And neither can you. We're not liberated for the better. Maybe for the worse.
Mayakovsky	Where will you go?
Osip	Maybe to a monastery.
Mayakovsky	They've closed the monasteries and taken the church land. You can't take Lily to a monastery. You don't know anything about monasteries.
Osip	We can stay with relatives and wait out the war.
Mayakovsky	I'll go to the mountains.
Osip	You can come with us.
Mayakovsky	No.
Osip	Come with us to the country.
Mayakovsky	No. I'll visit the Caucasus.
Osip	Fine. But you'd better do it soon. The lines are being drawn. Everybody will be fighting everybody else. And they'll all be drunk.

Scene 15

A picnic in the Kremlin. You can see the spacing. Stalin and Nadja knee to knee. Voroshilov far enough away.

Stalin   Voroshilov. Look what's happened. Our men are out on the streets.

Nadja   I can't stand these people, Koba.

"Koba" was Stalin's nickname in revolutionary days. Nadja often used the term. Voroshilov was one of his pals. Nadja breaks in:

Nadja   I can't stand the way they dress. The way they talk. The way they think. The way they lie. I can't stand anything about them. The way they eat. The way they talk. The way they drink.

Stalin   Why so harsh?

Nadja   I am a social revolutionary, like you. I can speak however I want to.

Stalin   It doesn't become you.

Nadja   Oh, I left out the stupid drinking.

Stalin   No, you didn't.

Nadja   So, I'm done.

Stalin   The Red Army is winning the cities, Nadja. The Red Army has won.

Nadja   The world is run by gangsters. Gangsters win and gangsters lose.

Stalin   There's no good to be found in it, Nadja?

Nadja   None.

Stalin   Thank you.

Nadja   You're welcome.

Stalin   What more do you want?

Nadja	A moment's peace. That sounds so precious. You probably have no idea what I mean. I don't care about the world. It is going to hell. It's me I care about. It's my insides. Not to be badgering myself, criticizing myself, feeling sorry for myself, hating myself. Do you follow?
Stalin	You need to get out more, Nadja. See people, see your friends, do things.
Nadja	Like what?
Stalin	I don't know. Make an effort.
Nadja	I don't feel like making an effort. But I see that I have to. Make an effort. *(Pause)* A certain effort has to be made. I have to make an effort. Effort. *(Pause)* I need to be myself.
Stalin	I agree.
Nadja	Do you have any idea who that is? What kind of effort? Who are we speaking of? Who is myself? What is myself? This piece of fertilizer I call myself?
Stalin	You are a wife, a daughter, a mother, a sister, a friend, a member of society, a Communist, and a creative intellectual, with duties and obligations and roles to play. And you have to play them.
Nadja	Why?
Stalin	For historical reasons.
Nadja	And then you die.
Stalin	Yes.
Nadja	And that's it?
Stalin	It's enough.
Nadja	For the atheists among us, it would seem so, yes. Communists.

Stalin	Yes. It's enough for us. We are the Vanguard.
Nadja	Excuse me. And for the religious? You don't have to tell me. Russians are Christians. Ask Masha. For them, there's another world. If you fulfill yourself. And obey the Church.
Stalin	A false God. I have studied it. Seriously. I should know.
Nadja	All the religions are wrong?
Stalin	I don't know about all the religions. All I know is we have made a Revolution, and the church has no more power. Well and good for all.
Nadja	They can be very strict.
Stalin	Who can?
Nadja	The religions.
Stalin	Yes, no more of all that superstition in Russia. We are building a new world, Nadja, and we need everyone to pitch in. You, as well. No layabouts or dreamers. No absconders. No cowards. People who can work and hold their heads high. Men who can bear the weight of hard labor and fight for their homeland, and make sacrifices.
Nadja	Women, too?
Stalin	Women, too. Of course.
Nadja	That sounds totally insane. *(Pause)*
Stalin	What did you say?
Nadja	Nothing, Koba. I was thinking out loud.
Stalin	Excuse me, Nadja. I need to talk with the Comrade.
Nadja	You're excused.

Stalin	Don't stay in your room all the time. Get out and do things. Visit hospitals. Go to meetings. Help the poor.
Nadja	Right.
	He stands. Hesitates.
Stalin	And your mother?
Nadja	What about her?
Stalin	How is she?
Nadja	Why do you ask?
Stalin	Good woman. A true and loyal Communist.
Nadja	Yes. I should take more after her.
Stalin	Yes, you should. See you in a moment. Come, Voroshilov.
	He looks off into the future, waves a finger to his patient friend, Voroshilov, who crosses downstage to join him. In the background, Nadja contemptuously watches them, then walks slowly away.

END ACT 1

Act 2

Scene 16

Speaks the Sincere Intellectual:

Stalin There is no God. Not for us. In the cemetery—I meant to say, "seminary"—there was only recitation and discipline, recitation and discipline. Repetition. Repetition and the slap on your hand with a mean stick. So I learned something there. How to be quiet. How to be unseen. And of course, I learned to read. There, I found Marx and Engels, and I learned to be obscure. How not to show myself too bright or too dim.

And then I'd had enough of their false ideology and became true to the Russian Revolution. I learned how to print leaflets, how to shout in a mob, how to fight with my fists, how to hide, how to steal, how to shoot, how to be bold and ruthless. I learned how to argue, how to make a case. How to act like a Russian. How to drink vodka and talk drunk with the comrades. How ennobling is the training from the Party, the real thing, not academic, but learned in the streets! How to bear privation, penury, starvation, torture! Abuse by petty tyrants! Being hunted like a mad dog! Confined like a wild animal! And so to enjoy freedom, freedom of movement, freedom of expression! And to enjoy one's comrades in the cause!

Later, I learned even to enjoy the cold of Siberia. Daily it could be twenty below. I shot bears. I caught fish to eat and boiled infested barley. Even the few rubles I

begged from the comrades in Baku went a long way.
I always paid it back, and more. One survives. One
holds fast and triumphs in the name of reason.
As for God, there is no Old Man in the sky watching
over us, Jewish no less, with his little beanie and his
white beard. No. Sometimes, in the morning, in
Siberia, in the cold and the dark, I would feel a
striving, like a fire in the chest, a feeling of destiny,
yes, a feeling of destiny, as though my life were
important and had meaning, historically, for the right
and the just. Lenin would chuckle at that, and slap
my back—but, it's true, so I felt. A calling. A
vocation. Nothing, of course, could stand in my way.
Nothing could have a higher valuation then the
achievement and maintenance of a true Revolution.
And so it stands.

Joseph Stalin.

Stalin.

*The Man of Steel.has made a rare visit to Nadja's little
bedroom. He's uncomfortable amidst all the white
linen, mirrors, and lace.*

Stalin	Machines. We are talking about machines. We are not talking about spirits. We are not talking about souls. Machines. History. History drives the machines.
Nadja	History is our God?
Stalin	Call it whatever you want. Struggle, if you want. Conflict. War. Whatever you want.
Nadja	I don't want any of it.
Stalin	You don't know what you want, Nadja.
Nadja	You don't know, either—

Stalin	We are not there yet.
Nadja	—What I want.
Stalin	Where we can talk about wants. Now we are creating the State. The State first. The mechanism of the State. Then we can talk about wants. Because the Revolution has come for us. The Revolution has intervened.
Nadja	Murder and fear and secret plotting, Koba. You like that sort of thing. You know exactly what *you* want.
Stalin	I like planning. Planning for the future. Otherwise, everything is random, accidental, in the hands of the royals and the rich, who benefit from ignorance, who take advantage of the workers and the poor. The Revolution starts a new way, a new, organized approach to life, to History. The first thing is the worker's State.
Nadja	You keep saying that. I've heard it a hundred times. The State and the Party are one.
Stalin	Because it's true. The Party must lead, the Party must govern, and one man must stand for the Party. At the moment, that man is myself. We have no choice. We ARE the revolution, Nadja. It seems clear as day to me. And we must keep to its path.
Nadja	*(To herself)* Oh! I'm so worried about that!
Stalin	We are doing it now, as we speak. The Red Army has secured the borders. We begin industrializing to scale. We'll soon develop a new agriculture. The Party is fit and trim and prepared to execute its mission.
Nadja	To execute?

Stalin	Yes, to function and administrate, to support the revolutionary cause, worldwide. You see that I do work with others. There are others with me, all over the world, who are on my side.
Nadja	*(You have no real friends, Koba.)*
Stalin	As long as we are together.
Nadja	*(Your only friend is the State.)*
Stalin	There'll be a new way of living, a new social structure, a new happiness, Nadja . . . there's the hope. There's hope for the future.
Nadja	Did you hear yourself just now? I would kill myself if I heard myself say things like that.
Stalin	Cowardice, Nadja. Spend more time with your friends.
Nadja	I have no friends.
Stalin	We must be careful.
Nadja	Only the maid, and she's a spy.
Stalin	We have sacrificed our lives, Nadja. Let's accept that. For the sake of the future.
Nadja	The hell with the future.
Stalin	We have to live.
Nadja	This is not living.
Stalin	What else would you do?
Nadja	This is a prison.
Stalin	Where else would you go?
Nadja	Out.
Stalin	There is no way out for us, and no way back.
Nadja	When we were in the railcar at Tsaritsyn, you remember?
Stalin	Yes.

Nadja	We were together, we were equal, we were in the battle together.
Stalin	Yes.
Nadja	And now?
Stalin	Now the situation has changed. Now we are in power.
Nadja	What is my place now?
Stalin	At my side.
Nadja	No, I sit quietly in my room. Or I pretend to preside over the children. I'm not even invited to dinner with the boys.
Stalin	It's business. You wouldn't like it.
Nadja	Drunken idiots. Buffoons.
	He goes to the window and looks toward the West and the setting sun, muttering to himself:
Stalin	I have no stomach for all this pathological thinking. She must pull herself together.

Scene 17

Another day. As Stalin and Kirov walk the Kremlin grounds. It's snowing. Snow. The strange phenomenon of snow.

Kirov	What a place the earth is, with its rain and snow, and molten iron in the center. It gives one pause.
Stalin	Kirov. People have to give up the idea that this movement can go forward without the institution of harsh measures.
Kirov	Yes, Comrade.
Stalin	Party leaders must give up their security.

Kirov	But there is danger, sir. There are counter-revolutionaries everywhere. Tribal forces. Religious fanatics. The Western powers.
Stalin	I don't mean that. I mean their personal security. Their comfort. Their psychology. They get too secure in their positions, and then they are no longer of use to the aims of the Party, which are ruthless aims. Impersonal aims. We are installing a new agriculture, a new industrial complex, a new political system. This is not child's play.
Kirov	History is not ready for it. There will be continued resistance.
Stalin	We are the Vanguard. We must keep to our aims. Surrounded by enemies, inside and out. Resentments, jealousies, ambitions. We will defeat them one by one. You must be resolute.
Kirov	I am, sir. We are strong now at the center, in the party apparatus. You have taken custody of Lenin's program. Everything good flows from that, from the leadership. Determined and unwavering.
Stalin	Right, Kirov. Quite right.
Kirov	What are you proposing, sir?
Stalin	Nothing big, Kirov. Just to disturb some party leaders a little. Why? I don't like being worried about what goes on in other people's heads. I know what's going on in mine. And I know what's going on in theirs. People are fearful of their status. People are fearful of their rights. For their next meal, for love and admiration, and so on.

Kirov	Of course.
Stalin	That can change, when we succeed. We can have everything we want then. It could take fifty, a hundred years. With courage, and time, and sacrifice, we will win. It's historically inevitable.
Kirov	Of course.
Stalin	Stop saying that. "Of course, of course."
Kirov	Sorry, Sir.
Stalin	Comrade.
Kirov	Comrade.
Stalin	Just listen. Pay attention. As far as the West goes, they will disintegrate on their own, crushed by their capitalist and degenerate fantasies. And by our strength. And the women, the Russian women.
Kirov	(*Surprised*) The women?
Stalin	Yes. I'm thinking about them. They must have a path to advancement in the Party.
Kirov	They do now, sir. Comrade.
Stalin	Not enough. We must make the path wider, easier for them.
Kirov	Yes. That would be ideal.
Stalin	Especially the white ones, the Caucasians. The true Russians. Now we have too many Jews in the hierarchy. We must gradually get rid of them.
Kirov	They have always been with us, Comrade.
Stalin	I know. They are some of the founders of the Party. So that's the way it is for now.
Kirov	And then there are Arabs on our borders. Muslim nationalists, sir.

Stalin	I've seen them. They are in our Party also. And I grew up around them. In the Caucasus, it was said that the women fuck with dogs.
Kirov	Comrade?
Stalin	Ha, ha. Behind their niqabs and black sheets. Just a joke, Kirov.
Kirov	They do present a threat, sir.
Stalin	The women?
Kirov	No, the Muslim nationalists. Like the Chechens, the Uzbeks, the Khazaks.
Stalin	I know all that, Comrade. I was once Minister to the Minorities. When Lenin was alive.
Kirov	I remember, Sir.
Stalin	We will protect our borders, now that they are secure. And create buffer zones all around. Areas where no one can live in peace. All around us, so we can thrive within. Let's get back to the women. What do you think about that?
Kirov	I agree. Even in the army. Our women would make excellent soldiers. We are a secular nation. No reason they shouldn't serve.
Stalin	In the old days, they stayed in their place. Religion and society. I mean the women. They worked in the kitchen, they brought up the kids, they went to church and all that. Now? Now they must have a voice. I studied for the priesthood, you know, in Tiflis, but I came to see religion as false. I became a Marxist and a brigand. I am interested in the real world. *(Pause)* Where was I?
Kirov	The real world.

Stalin	The real world. Which has meaning, finally, don't you think? It's because there is something above me—the Party—the forces of dialectical materialism. Class war, the dictatorship of the proletariat—and so on. At last, there is meaning.
Kirov	Yes, at last. I agree, Comrade Stalin.

Kirov shudders, as though from a chill. He has realized that his head is perched delicately upon his neck.

Scene 18

Nadja is riding in the back seat of an American car on a gray Russian country road. A movie camera mounted on a sidecar is rolling alongside it. Stalin sits in front with the driver. Nadja looks out at the camera.

Nadja	Drop dead, *she says.* You are History's spy.

Stalin stares straight in front of him. At the windshield. It's hard to tell if he's thinking anything. He never looks like he's thinking.

Nadja	What is he thinking? *Says Nadja to herself.*

He looks like he's blank inside. Like there's nothing going on in there. That's how he looks.

Nadja	But there's a lot going on in there. Scheming and plotting.

We don't know. We don't know what was going on in there.

Maybe he was meditating.

Maybe he was praying.

Maybe he was dreaming.

Maybe there was nothing going on in there.

Nadja looks at the camera: An appendage of the State, a watcher of the State, recording the History of the State, the awakening of the Worker's State, the Man of Steel on the country road, not smiling, Nadja in the back looking at the camera: He's nice to his kids, she says, he's not a bad guy, if you looked at him you wouldn't know if he was thinking anything. You can't tell by looking at people what they are, what they're thinking. You can't tell. Faces lie. He gives away nothing. He is hidden in there by his face, the Sincere Intellectual.

There was a next moment. We don't know what it was. Everything we know is from the movies. In those days the movies were new, photography was new, but Nadja was on to it, Nadja was hip to it, Nadja was sick of the whole thing, sick and tired of the whole thing, the show business of the Soviet Empire, while Stalin sits impassively in front thinking nothing and the camera rolls, and the driver drives, and they come to a palace and go into the palace, and Stalin says something, and people run around, and Nadja goes to her room, and they park the car, and nothing comes of the whole thing.

Only History.

Of which we know next to nothing. Nothing is left of the past except a few bones. A few photographs, a few bricks, a few words on paper.

The bones of Nadja, the bones of Stalin, the bones of Mayakovsky. The bones of Lily and Osip Brik.

We know almost nothing of the past, almost nothing of the future. This is all we know.

Stalin grunts as they arrive at the Kremlin: "That is correct."

Nadja goes into her room in the palace. She touches lace. Everything is white. Why a palace? This is a Worker's State. It's a palace. She touches lace. The Mauser is hidden under a maroon pillow. The silken cover is embroidered with the Red Star.

Nadja   My body is a piece of meat, *she thinks,* bleeding once a month, that's all I'm here for, and I don't like my face. I don't think it's fair to me, because I have consciousness. I have thinking. I have self-awareness. That's what they mean by suffering your sins. In Russia. In old Russia. You suffered for your sins. Including mistreatment of the serfs. Cruelty to the serfs. I was not a serf. I don't know what I was. I had a nice life.

Nadja listens to the radio and looks at her face. Her face is changing. It is no longer the same face.

Nadja   I am Nadja. A young woman. Bourgeois? You can imagine. Gorillas in the dining room. At my age, you begin to sense a little about death and dying. Suffering and decay. Inevitable and soon. Imagine. Movies are a big deal. So is the radio. Did Lenin like the movies? I'll have to look it up. Who doesn't like the movies? You can check out of this life for a couple of hours.

There is a mirror everywhere she looks.

Nadja   I don't see my face. I don't see my face at all. It is losing its shape, it is losing its color. (*Masha appears behind her.*)

Nadja   Masha. How do I look?

Masha   You look fine.

Nadja	I look the same?
Masha	You look the same.
Nadja	I don't feel the same. Too many things have happened. Too much wear and tear.
Masha	You look fine, you look great.
Nadja	You're lying.
Masha	I'm not lying. You can't see yourself.
Nadja	I can't see myself at all. Not even in the mirror. All these mirrors, and I am blind to myself. How can that be?
Masha	God doesn't want us to suffer too much.
Nadja	What did you say?
Masha	Nothing.
Nadja	And you? How do you look?
Masha	I look my age. I'm grey and pinched and a little hunched-over, like an old bird.
Nadja	You don't look so bad, Masha. And you've had a hard life. You're an ignorant peasant. I take that back. You're a serious, educated woman. You're a bona fide obyvatel. I was too, once. Don't ask me when. What do you believe in, Masha?
Masha	I believe in God and Religion.
Nadja	Look at the lines, creeping around my eyes, my mouth. The flesh is starting to die.
Masha	All flesh dies. It's what's inside that matters, Madam.
Nadja	Nothing's inside.
Masha	The spirit. The soul. God is in you.
Nadja	Look at me and tell me the truth.
Masha	You look fine, Madam.
Nadja	Don't lie like that in front of your God.
Masha	You look sad.

Nadja	I'm going to kill myself.
Masha	Don't even think such thoughts.
Nadja	You can control your thoughts, Masha?
Masha	I pray. I pray. I pray.
Nadja	This helps you?
Masha	Yes. It holds my mind in the right direction.
Nadja	Good for you.
Masha	You're still a beautiful woman, Madam, with beautiful children. I wouldn't worry so much.
Nadja	Thanks, Masha. On the radio they are talking politics and statecraft, and in the other room about murdering people who are not getting with the program of the State apparatus. Mean, shifty-eyed, bulky people in dark clothes, watching Stalin's face and murmuring lies and cracking stupid dirty jokes.
Masha	I'm sorry to hear it, Ma'am.
Nadja	Say "comrade."
Masha	I'm sorry, Comrade.
Nadja	Go away, Masha.

Masha glimpses herself as she tiptoes out of the mirrored room. She is a slim, dark, sharp-eyed woman. Well-dressed, professional. A moment of fear. A moment of regret.

Scene 19

Mayakovsky is drunk in front of a horde of drunken workers in a Russian town where people don't know much poetry except for sentimental folk songs.

| Mayakovsky | Yet each man kills the thing he loves, |

By each let this be heard,
Some do it with a bitter look,
Some with a flattering word,
The coward does it with a kiss,
The brave man with a sword. *(Pause)*
And so on and so forth.

Mayakovsky continues to his audience of workers and students:

Mayakovsky   What do you think about that, you assholes? You apes! While the politicians steal what's left of your minds, your decency, your stupid dreams. Get to work! Work, work, work! This is a worker's State! At least we don't fuck around with God anymore! Am I right? You're not sure? You don't know? A bunch of clowns! Gangsters! Bad things are coming, Lily. Bad things are coming fast. The earth is a murder factory. And the cause could be in the sun, in the moon, in the atmosphere, in the soil, in the blood.

Lily rises, and makes a face.

Lily   I can't be with you when you're like this, Volodya.

Mayakovsky   Then go away.

She moves toward the door, catches herself in the mirror, checks herself out, half-smiles, pivots.

Lily   No.

Mayakovsky   Look around you, Lily. The age of the industrial machine. There'll come a time, we won't need people anymore. No, that's not right. We'll be the machines. And we'll break. That's the way it will be. Very efficient, very productive. Until we break.

Lily   Not like you.

Mayakovsky	No, not like me. They'll get rid of machines like me, who are already broken.
Lily	And me.
Mayakovsky	Yes. They'll kill all the clowns. *(Music/Crescendo)* **Get off the stage!** *The Workers shout back.*
Lily	Volodya, let's get out of here! *Lily is calling to him. He's trying to talk to the so-called proletariat. Meanwhile everybody was killing everybody else. A bloody free-for-all, with plenty of vodka flowing through the pipes. You could go on a rampage and forget about tomorrow. Various armies were forming around the entire country. They almost strung up our Mayakovsky in a drunken riot.*
Lily	I can't go on like this.
Mayakovsky	Yes, you can.
Lily	No. I can't do it.
Mayakovsky	So, good. You go your way, and I'll go back to the Caucasus.
Lily	And when you get there?
Mayakovsky	I'll crop hay and write poems.
Lily	I'm the best friend you have in the world, Volodya. I listen to you well.
Mayakovsky	Not enough. Never mind. It's my own fault. I fall in love like a puppet. The puppets are loose in Mother Russia. The strings are cut and nobody knows where they belong. Only you don't seem to care, because of your good looks.
Lily	I hold them dear.
Mayakovsky	As well you should.
Lily	I'm intelligent. I intend to survive.

Mayakovsky	Good for you. Otherwise, there is no other intelligence at work. The earth has shaken its skin and the cracks are open straight to hell. It's all greed and vodka and stupidity and people screaming bloody murder. So far.
Lily	What did you expect? A Revolution is a Revolution.
Mayakovsky	That's what Lenin thinks. He has one thought, and he thinks it's right. No matter the cost. That's what your husband thinks, too.
Lily	I'm going to the country with my husband.
Mayakovsky	To escape the New World Order?
Lily	To escape the Red Army. To escape the White Army. To escape all the armies.
Mayakovsky	I told Osip already, I am not coming with you.
Lily	Where will you go?
Mayakovsky	Wherever they play cards.
Lily	Who will take care of you?
Mayakovsky	I don't need anyone to take care of me.
Lily	I'm afraid you do.
Mayakovsky	Why didn't you become a mother, Lily?
Lily	I'm not a mother. My mother was a mother, and that was enough. And why bring a child into this chaos?
Mayakovsky	There, you agree with me. Random chaos. A million ways to suffer and die. Hopefully, things will get better.
Lily	You can do better—you can come with us.
Mayakovsky	You get up and wash your face and get through the day. And at the end you look back with regret. Isn't that the way of it? No. I won't come with you.
Lily	Volodya.

Mayakovsky	Or you go to the movies. The flickering image of another world, even less real then the one we're in.
Lily	It's only an image. A trick of lighting. You see it in your poetry. It's the way your mind works.
Mayakovsky	I think on the page. I make mistakes. The line must have integrity. The image must have integrity. And sometimes they don't. Too much like the chaos of life, where the only certainty is sickness and death.
Lily	What about the simple pleasures, Volodya, like sex and food, music and companionship?
Mayakovsky	I think they do count.
Lily	Good.
Mayakovsky	Of course they count. One must live. One must live and more than live. And give our best to the Revolution. Old Caucasian saying.

Scene 20

It's 1918. Stalin is holed up in a railroad car in Baku, gathering grain for Lenin in Moscow. He had decided to shoot anyone who disagreed with him. It worked. He got plenty of grain for the leader. Nadja, it turns out, was there with him on the train.

Nadja	You're my hero. (They embrace roughly.) Don't love me too hard, and don't let anyone else in on it.
Stalin	We're man and wife. We were married by the commissar. Totally legal. No one can interfere with us. I'll have them shot.
Nadja	You're having everybody shot.
Stalin	If you don't shoot them, they won't listen.

Nadja	If you shoot them, they won't listen then, either. Basic Communist sense, Koba.
Stalin	This is it. This is a turning point. No food, no Revolution, no Communism, no Motherland.
Nadja	How do you decide who dies?
Stalin	They get in my way, I kill them.
Nadja	So what did you do? You put up a list?
Stalin	Yes. First I put up a list. I post it. If there's any trouble, and they're on the list to be shot, I have them shot.
Nadja	It's unbelievable.
Stalin	I publish the list. So it comes as no surprise.
Nadja	Still, there's trouble.
Stalin	I have a starting point, but I don't stop there. I go on from there. I have an arsenal here. Give me the grain, that's all you need to know. The man sent me to do a job. We're making history. There's armed militias running around all over the area. Everybody's got a gun. This is Baku. They got oil here. Right and left. It's sitting right on the ground. One day it'll come in handy. It's waiting for us, like all these fools waiting for Koba to come and kill them. Getting out of the way. Do you follow me?
Nadja	No. I don't follow you.
Stalin	Out of the way of History. It's not politics now. It's Revolution now.
Nadja	Yes. And we're married now.
Stalin	Yes!
Nadja	How do we know?
Stalin	It's in writing, Nadja. Because I signed the document, me and the commissar. I am the steel pen of History.

	I am the knife. The Doer. We are married for good. For life. Think of that, Nadja! No priests, no bureaucrats! Let's have a cuddle, Nadja.
Nadja	Good, get rid of all these drunken bums, and I'll think it over.
Stalin	*(To the Crowd:)* Out! Out! *(Noises off)*
Nadja	So we can have some privacy in here. And put some coal on the fire. And round up some soup, so we can have something to eat. Eh, Great One?
Stalin	For you—anything, doll.
	A pause while the Great One stokes the fire.
Nadja	What did you do to Ekatarina?
	Stalin bends over like he's been beaten across the back, and shows his teeth and growls, like a dog. His knee knocks into the little stove.
Stalin	Damn. Nothing, Nadja. I did nothing to Ekatarina.
Nadja	Were you there?
Stalin	You know where I was. I was working. For the party.
Nadja	Robbing and killing and telling lies, no doubt, for the local population.
Stalin	Yes. And spending some time in prison, too.
Nadja	And Ekatarina?
Stalin	I've told you before. She was sick.
Nadja	You told me. Yes. Sick. And a loyal Communist.
Stalin	Always.
Nadja	I come from Communist stock too, you know.
Stalin	Yes, you have very good breeding, Nadja. But Communism is not in the blood.
Nadja	How do you know?

Stalin	It's not the kind of passion that is passed through the body alone. It is hard-earned and made body and soul, and with the mind. My father was a simple shoemaker.
Nadja	I know. This is not the right time for a cuddle.
Stalin	No. Too many scoundrels lurking around here. Let's wait.
Nadja	Yes. Now that we're married, we can wait.
	And the question of Ekaterina can wait, too.
	The Revolutionary train moves on.

Scene 21

Lily	This is the age of the Futurists.
Mayakovsky	This is the future.
Lily	There is no future.
Mayakovsky	It's propaganda.
Lily	There is no future, Volodya.
Mayakovsky	It's propaganda.
Lily	Bodies turning to dust, becoming the air we breathe.
Mayakovsky	I am thinking about it.
Lily	What could they have possibly been thinking?
Mayakovsky	It's propaganda.
Lily	There's nothing left. Stones and bones.
Mayakovsky	Stones and bones.
Lily	Everything is moving at astronomical speed.
Mayakovsky	And yet we live. And hope.
Lily	And make plans.
Mayakovsky	And they do have the idea of Utopia, these people.
Lily	Say what you want to say.
Mayakovsky	Everybody is going to die!
Lily	You said that. It doesn't mean anything.

Mayakovsky	You're pissing me off now. You can't understand what I'm trying to say. Are you suddenly stupid? *(Pause)* Utopia. I'll tell you what's going to happen, okay?
Lily	Tell, tell.
Mayakovsky	What always happens. People will degenerate into what they really are. Stupid and self-serving beasts. They'll do anything and believe anything. They'll run around on their horses and ride trains, yelling and screaming and raising hell. That's what they like to do.
Lily	You think it was better with the Czar?
Mayakovsky	No. They were fighting a lost war in the West. We had no chance. They had spies everywhere. The economy was falling apart. The people wanted a change. They're still on the streets. And they're armed. Mindlessly. Now it might be too late for anything good to happen.
Lily	Don't drink too much.
Mayakovsky	Can I open my mouth?
Lily	Are you asking me?
Mayakovsky	Can I open my mouth?
Lily	Talk, Volodya.
Mayakovsky	I'm talking.
Lily	Talk.
Mayakovsky	What's wrong with these people? Uniforms and guns. Everyone will have a piece of bread and a place to sleep. Beautiful little hands will feed you grapes and coffee in the morning. And butter! Pink clouds will bring soft rain. Golden corn will grow on the Russian steppes. God will be in his castle. Happiness will rule the land.
Lily	You're drunk.

Mayakovsky	I'm not drunk, the commissars are drunk. They have opened fire on the people. What fun! It's unbelievable what fun you can have these days! Torturing! Raping teen-agers! I'd like to get in on that myself. All you have to do is be right and say the right words and have a gun or a cannon or a whip. People do not think. People do not reason. People want to be saved. People want to take what they want. Wheat! All you need is wheat!
Lily	You're incoherent, Volodya.
Mayakovsky	People say things and they have no idea what they're saying! This world will end in a fart. The fart of a blind old man. Like Lear. Farting in the wind. As much horseshit as can fit in his belly—he farts it out and the whole of Russia stinks like a corpse!
Lily	Society will keep it in check. There are rules and customs. There are civilized people in the world.
Mayakovsky	You watch and see, Lilyana. Watch and see.

Scene 22

Stalin	Masha! *(Silence)* Masha! *(Enter Masha)*
Masha	Yes, Master?
Stalin	Don't call me Master.
Masha	What shall I call you?
Stalin	Call me Comrade.
Masha	Yes, sir.
Stalin	Sir is good, sir is fine. What's wrong with my wife, Masha?
Masha	Nothing, sir.

Stalin	There is no such thing as nothing. Everything is something.
Masha	Yes, sir.
Stalin	Do you follow me?
Masha	I think so.
Stalin	What did I say?
Masha	There is no such thing as nothing.
Stalin	Exactly. So answer my question.
Masha	Nothing, sir, is the matter. (That is a lie.)
Stalin	You know I almost became a priest? You know that?
Masha	No, sir.
Stalin	Nadja never told you?
Masha	Not me, sir.
Stalin	In Tiflis. I was a teen-ager. Much was discussed about substance and nothing. Transubstantiation. So I know what I'm talking about. I know the difference. That's why I am who I am. You know that. A sincere and devoted Communist intellectual. Yes?
Masha	Yes. (Sincere and devoted.)
Stalin	So what's going on with her? I'll tell you. She thinks too much when she should be doing practical things. Serving the Party. Serving the cause. Seeing to the children. What is she thinking about? People are wondering. People are guessing. We don't want that. We don't need to have that kind of thing going on around here. This is the Kremlin, this is the center of all our activities. So tell me something that is not nothing. *(Silence)* Masha?
Masha	She tries to live her life as best she can.
Stalin	So what's the problem?

Masha	She needs more time, sir.
	What does she do?, thinks Koba, what the fuck does she do?
Masha	She's very intelligent.
Stalin	More time?
Masha	Yes.
Stalin	I see. Thank you. You might remind her, Masha, that she has responsibilities, responsibilities to me, and to the Party, and to her children, and so on. Talk to her, Masha. About real things. She listens to you. Real historical questions. Not domestic anxieties. Nothing personal. You understand?
Masha	I think so.
Stalin	Good. Thank you, Masha.
Masha	Good day to you, sir.

Scene 23

Somewhere on the Pale of Settlement, where the Jews were allowed to live, on the Western steppes of Russia, years ago, Lily Brik and her sister, Elsa, are traveling home:

Elsa	Why do you wash yourself all the time?
Lily	I don't.
Elsa	You do.
Lily	When I travel.
Elsa	You always do. You do it constantly.
Lily	It's because of the human stink. *(Pause)* There's nothing to be ashamed of. *(Pause)* The urge to be clean and nice.

Elsa	And that tall pig, Mayakovsky. The poet. I don't like him. He's an animal.
Lily	He is a poet. A good one. But he has doubts. About himself, about the Revolution. He takes it all personally.
Elsa	But why do you associate with him?
Lily	Because there's nothing else to do. To find something intelligent, something beautiful. The trouble is, he doesn't like himself. You and I, we're almost normal. We live our lives and don't worry about it too much. But Volodya, he suffers. The "Evil Empire" is on its way. *Mayakovsky supported the New—a new politics, a new Art, a new Future, a new Society. But it was not to be quite that way.*
Elsa	I'm leaving this country.
Lily	When?
Elsa	As soon as I can.

Scene 24

Volodya, Lily. The samovar. Cigarettes. Booze. Sounds from the Moscow streets.

Mayakovsky	Nice to see you.
Lily	Thank you.
Mayakovsky	Already I sense a vibration.
Lily	Really?
Mayakovsky	Yes, of correspondence, compatibility.
Lily	Horseshit.
Mayakovsky	Desire. What is that?
Lily	Reproduction.

Mayakovsky	It's rare. Electricity. Polar nodes attract.
Lily	How interesting.
Mayakovsky	We must act.
Lily	Not today.
Mayakovsky	Why not?
Lily	I'm tired.
Mayakovsky	You're not tired.
Lily	I am tired.
Mayakovsky	I only get it up when I'm near you.
Lily	Really? Put it in the icebox.
Mayakovsky	That's the only time.
Lily	Really. Take a cold shower.
Mayakovsky	Otherwise, I have no interest.
Lily	I don't believe you.
Mayakovsky	It's an electro-chemical event.
Lily	Causes too many problems.
Mayakovsky	Actually, I'm glad when it happens. I feel alive. I feel manly. *(Pause)* You're a cock-tease.
Lily	Sorry. Not happening. Not today. *(Pause)*
Mayakovsky	So I might rape you.
Lily	I don't think so.
Mayakovsky	I'm thinking about it.
Lily	No, no, Volodya.
Mayakovsky	Why not?
Lily	It would ruin our relationship.
Mayakovsky	What relationship?
Lily	Of love.
Mayakovsky	What love?
Lily	Based on respect. Find a whore, Volodya. They're all over the place these days. Nice women. The economy is crumbling. They might enjoy it. And they need the money.

Mayakovsky	I have no money.
Lily	Where's the money?
Mayakovsky	I lost it at the casino.
Lily	Oh, Volodya!
Mayakovsky	Don't change the subject.
Lily	You have to stop that!
Mayakovsky	I agree.
Lily	I'll loan you the money.
Mayakovsky	Never mind.
Lily	Now I have to go.
Mayakovsky	Where?
Lily	To rehearse. It's *The Bed Bug*, your own play. You should be glad.
Mayakovsky	I am.
Lily	You should be there.
Mayakovsky	But it's a lousy play.
Lily	It's a very good play.
Mayakovsky	Thank you. I don't feel up to it.
Lily	Suit yourself. Bye, bye.
Mayakovsky	Bye! I love you!
	And she blows him a kiss and dances out of the room. La di da.

Scene 25

Stalin stands at the window, looking west, hands clasped behind him. Once in a while he rocks slightly on his heels.

Nadja	Do you believe in God? Koba?
	Stalin rocks on his booted heels. Nadja tries again.
Nadja	Did you hear me?
Stalin	What kind of question is that?

Nadja	A simple question.
Stalin	You know I don't.
Nadja	You went to seminary.
Stalin	Everyone went to seminary. That's where we learned.
Nadja	What did you learn?
Stalin	The meaning of God.
Nadja	Which is?
Stalin	To distract the masses from their actual situation.
Nadja	And you?
Stalin	To clear the Way. Don't ask me to what, but I'm going to tell you anyway—to a world where everyone—
Nadja	Is at fault?—
Stalin	No. Equal. And free of superstition and false obedience. Where everyone knows his place and what to do. Where no one is lording it over them.
Nadja	Except you.
Stalin	Except me, for the moment. There has to be unity. One, from the top. The very top-most branch. One voice. One authority. Otherwise, there is chaos, and nobody knows what to do. Someone right away must make the really difficult decisions. Right away.
Nadja	Who lives, who dies.
Stalin	That is correct, Nadja. We are talking about reality, now.
Nadja	I am talking about reality.
Stalin	No, you are dreaming.
Nadja	I don't think so. I am not dreaming.
Stalin	You are dreaming.
Nadja	So what if I am. So what?
Stalin	We don't need dreams, dreams are for sleeping people—we need action.

Nadja	Lies like the Socialist Soviet Republic. What do you care about the people? You don't care one molecule about the people.
Stalin	The people are what we mean by History, Nadja. People and work. Economics. Health. Education.
Nadja	You are not serious.
Stalin	We have made a serious Revolution, in the real world, and I am the spear point of that Revolution. At the moment.
	And the practical joker, too. He'd call someone and praise him and then crack open the person and have him shot the next day.
Nadja	Congratulations. I'm going to bed now.
Stalin	We don't live in a storybook, Nadja.
Nadja	No, we live in the hell of History. Tell me about Ekaterina.
Stalin	No.
Nadja	There's a real story there, I'm sure. From the real world.
Stalin	Go to bed.
Nadja	Liar!
Stalin	You are not well, Nadja.
	And he walks out of the room. He's good at that. "It's all I have to say. You tire me. See you some other time, if you're lucky. If you're worthy. If you deserve my attention."

Scene 26

Osip	Tell me again: why do you gamble so, Volodya?
Mayakovsky	I am not permitted to hold on to money, Osip.
Osip	Why not?

Mayakovsky	I don't deserve to be here like other people. I'm not allowed to be sick or have faults. Or friends. Or money.
Osip	Why not? You, a major poet and revolutionary intellectual.
Mayakovsky	My automatic mode is to feel small. Small in the sense of nothing.
Osip	You're a tall, handsome man.
Mayakovsky	I'm not athletic. I stumble and fall.
Osip	You drink too much.
Mayakovsky	Yes. And smoke too much. And gamble too much. And chase women too much.
Osip	Why? Why do all these things?
Mayakovsky	And think too much. *(Pause)* It makes me feel good for a minute.
Osip	None of my business.
Mayakovsky	Correct.
Osip	I envy you, actually. Women like you.
Mayakovsky	At first.
Osip	And then?
Mayakovsky	Well, my teeth are bad.
Osip	True. Your teeth are bad.
Mayakovsky	I talk too much and mumble.
Osip	Sometimes.
Mayakovsky	I overdo everything, and lose my shirt and pants and underwear and self-respect. Mainly my self-respect. My impulse is to bow. Like a monk, like a servant.
Osip	Why don't you, then?
Mayakovsky	It would be false, Osip. That would be silly. I'm not a believer, as you know.

Osip	You're a superior poet, Volodya.
Mayakovsky	Yes. I believe in poetry, apparently. If you can call it that. God knows why. And I believed in the Revolution. And in luck. Which I don't have. And my poetry is pretty bad, I think, for the most part, in the long run. And I look up to people. I look up to everybody.
Osip	You're too hard on yourself.
Mayakovsky	That's what your wife says. The freethinker. You're quoting her.
Osip	I think she's right.
Mayakovsky	I think so, too, Osip. That's part of the game of my life. That's why I gamble. Because I can't have anything and I can't endure anything. Even love.
Osip	We live in revolutionary times, Volodya, a time of big change.
Mayakovsky	I'll tell you what I suspect, Osip. *(Pause)* We are all shit. There'll be no change in that situation. People will do anything. In the circumstances. All they have to do is feel in the right. Believe. I don't trust anyone who believes too much.
Osip	You don't believe? In Art?
Mayakovsky	Art's okay. But most of it is shit. You're a nice Jewish boy, Osip. And I'm a nice little Cossack.
Osip	Speak for yourself.
Mayakovsky	Not so little and not so nice. But we both don't like violence and women intimidate us. Like Lilyana.
Osip	This is true. But I have reason. What about reason? It can help us to make our way. It's the language of the Enlightenment.

Mayakovsky	Look what it's brought us, Osip. Barbarism. I'm becoming afraid of these people in power now and I don't believe their lies anymore. They don't know what they're doing. But they think they're right. They have a cause. We act like deranged insects. Some in the name of God. God. Can you believe that? In this day and age? In the twentieth century? And not only God—in an idea about History. An idea. Killing for an idea!
Osip	I have hope. I still have hope.
Mayakovsky	In what?
Osip	In common sense, like I say. In reason. I'm going to the country until this madness subsides. We'll be the first fodder in the cannons. There are pogroms all over Russia. They are murdering Jews. In the West. In the East. We had all better lie low. Go to Switzerland, or Germany.
Mayakovsky	Good.
Osip	I'm taking Lily with me. Don't worry. The Czars are no longer with us. The serfs have been freed. New Men are forming who don't necessarily have to control their women.
Mayakovsky	Even love is a lie. A foolish delusion. A sexual nightmare. A carnal trap. I could go on, but never mind.
Osip	Goodbye, Volodya.
Mayakovsky	Very well, goodbye. That's enough of that.

Scene 27

Nadja has caught Stalin in the hallway. She speaks just above a whisper, as the comrades are not far behind them.

Nadja	Tell me about Ekaterina.
Stalin	I don't talk about Kato.
Nadja	Ekaterina. Kato?
Stalin	I don't talk about her. That was her nickname.
Nadja	She must have been the submissive type.
Stalin	She was sick.
Nadja	And a Red.
Stalin	She was Red.
Nadja	While you were robbing trains and killing people.
Stalin	For the Party.
Nadja	Yes, right. I remember now. She stayed home. But she was sick.
Stalin	She went along with it. She knew what I was doing.
Nadja	She died and it pissed you off.
Stalin	She died in my arms.
Nadja	I thought you were busy raiding and murdering and breaking into things.
Stalin	Yes, but I went to them finally, to Kato and her family. I came out of hiding and I managed to see them. *Nadja stops. Stalin stops. The comrades are not far behind. They stop, too, and pretend not to listen.*
Nadja	She died because of you. (Here is a person who is short and pockmarked with something wrong with him, like a fake limp, and a dark face, who thinks of himself as the sly and intellectual servant of the Communist cause. Actually, he is the psychotic son of a shoemaker. But women liked him. In the old days. God knows why. Maybe there's a soft look in his eye. No. He's determined. He's willing to kill. Are women attracted to that quality in a person? He believes in a cause. Maybe she was just stupid.) Was she stupid, Koba?

Stalin	Keep walking, Nadja.
	He takes her arm firmly and they walk. The comrades wait a moment, politely, and then follow.
Stalin	No, Kato was a Communist and good. A good person from a good family.
Nadja	Why did she die?
Stalin	Of an illness.
Nadja	What was the illness?
Stalin	Nobody knew what it was at the time. The doctors there, they were useless.
Nadja	It was you. You were the illness.
	Stalin had been sad and bewildered by his first wife's sickness. He and Ekaterina had got married in a church, much to the amusement of his fellow revolutionaries, including Trotsky, and they had had a little boy, whose name was Yakov.
Nadja	You're a believer. That's the trouble. Trouble comes from beliefs. Illness comes from belief.
Stalin	We must believe in something, or life's not worth living.
Nadja	But I don't believe in anything, Koba. So. Nothing more to say.
Stalin	Believe in reality, what you see around you.
Nadja	Why should I?
Stalin	Because it exists. It is the case.
Nadja	Here today, gone tomorrow.
Stalin	Not a joke. I want to live, like anyone else.
Nadja	Like any clever animal. You'll end up old and dying and bewildered. Your frightened comrades won't know what to do with your corpse. And you won't be able to

	tell them. The whole apparatus of the State will fall to pieces.
Stalin	It will not.
Nadja	It will have to. It's based on a lie.
Stalin	We have established institutions.
Nadja	Lies. That the State is good. That human nature is good. That goodness will prevail, that history is a reality, that time counts, that we make progress, that we are not insects. And so on.
Stalin	No, it's you. You've lost touch, Nadja, with the real world.
Nadja	I have not.
Stalin	I feel sorry for you.
Nadja	Feel whatever you like. I'm through with you.

Stalin stops and backs up a step to catch his breath and wait for his friends. Nadja continues on, whispering to herself, as though he were still beside her.

Nadja	Did she kiss your filthy mouth? Praise your scummy ideas? Wash your shitty underwear? Eh, Great One? Besides getting sick and staying out of your way, what else did she do for you? Oh, yes, she made lace!

Noticing that Stalin is now out of earshot, she shouts:

Nadja	You fuck-head! I promise you, there'll be mayhem and slaughter, because of you and your stupid ideas, your fanatic beliefs, but I won't be around to see it, no more, I promise you! I won't be here, you slimy piece of shit! I'll be gone!

Realizing her indiscretion, in front of the comrades, she concludes, softly:

Nadja	I'll be gone! *(Enter Masha)*

Masha	What's wrong, madam?
Nadja	Nothing. I was conversing with the Master. You don't have to follow me. Leave me alone.

A door opens and closes quietly. A sigh.

Scene 28

Nadja	Time is passing and I'm not there, Masha.
Masha	You must make use of the time. We only have so much time.
Nadja	You never know what will happen with a person.
Masha	No. No one knows.
Nadja	I don't feel like I'm here in time. I can't explain it.
Masha	There is so much to do, so much to be done.
Nadja	Not by me.
Masha	There are the children.
Nadja	They have nannies. Women who don't have bellies anymore. Why not? They don't use them. They live for other people's children. Anyway, I don't know how to be with children. I'm a Communist. Really, I am not even a Communist anymore.
Masha	You mustn't sit alone in your room. You must make appearances. What do the doctors say?
Nadja	About what? I don't need a rest. I want to do something.
Masha	Let's go to the country.
Nadja	Everyone wants to go to the country. What's in the country? It's so Russian. To want to go to the country. There's nothing there.
Masha	Peace and quiet, Nadja. A chance to rest.

Nadja	Beasts and vermin. I'll stay here in this room which is not a room. It's a dollhouse. They can burn it down if they want to. They're capable of anything. You can tell them to kill their mothers or to eat their children. *(Pause)* And they will. My husband will whisper in their ears, and they will do it. These are not fairy tales. We haven't seen the worst. I have dreams. You want to hear them? People are herded into ditches in the cold, protecting their private parts. They're shot there. When the authorities have run out of bullets, the people are buried alive and say, "thank you, God." Then their bodies are burned and their ashes are spread out all over the country. The peace and quiet of the country.
Masha	(God help us.)
Nadja	What do you do, Masha? Do you still pray?
Masha	Yes. I say my prayers. The usual prayers.
Nadja	I don't usually pray, myself. But I think it's good to have God on your side. Is God on your side?
Masha	Yes. And on your side, as well.
Nadja	That's good. Like a companion.
Masha	Yes.
Nadja	I don't usually talk about religion. Only with you. Don't tell the Master. Go ahead and pray, Masha. Pray for me. But don't let anyone see you. I have a disease. I hope your God can help Nadja. I don't know what he could possibly do. I have always served. I was born to serve.
Masha	(She is troubled in her mind, and there is nothing I can do.) Lord have mercy on us.

Nadja	Yes. I am a Communist. An ex-Communist. One of the first creatures of its kind on earth. Thank you, Masha. *They had telephones and photographs and movies and radio and the Theory of Relativity. Lily Brik thought she saw Einstein in an audience in Berlin.*

Scene 29

Masha	Allow me to summon a Holy Father, sir.
Stalin	What for?
Masha	He can give advice and comfort to your wife.
Stalin	What for?
Masha	For Nadja's soul.
Stalin	Nadja needs to buckle up and grab the reigns.
Masha	She needs meaning in her life, sir.
Stalin	Nadja is a Communist. She is in no need of any meaning. That is its own meaning. *(Pause)* You know what Communism is, don't you, Masha?
Masha	Yes, sir.
Stalin	It's not a religion. It is a creed, a way of life. No holy fathers, Masha. Nadja needs to participate, to get out more, to show herself to her people. She would enjoy that.
Masha	She wouldn't, sir.
Stalin	Well, too bad, then. She should study, write books, articles. Her parents were good at that sort of thing. But never mind—I'm tired of hearing about the whole thing. Let her be a mother to her children and not complain. Let her be useful to the Party. And come out of her silly room. You're paid handsomely to take

care of her needs, Masha, and to watch her, to watch her carefully, and to respond. You understand?

Masha Yes, sir.

Stalin Good. Then we're finished with this now. Go about your business, Masha.

Masha She's frightened, sir.

Stalin I didn't hear you.

Masha I said, she's frightened.

Stalin Of what?

Masha Of you, sir.

Stalin freezes. Maybe he takes a breath. Maybe he lights his pipe.

Stalin You want to keep your job, Masha?

Masha Yes, sir.

Stalin Then do your job. And then we'll see.

Stalin pivots and leaves. Masha knows—as we do— that bad things are going to happen. That the history of man is the history of slaughter, and that God can do nothing.

Scene 30

Mayakovsky The Futurists, they'll have brains without bodies. The brains will connect with other brains as smart as them—super brains. Together they will make a mega-god. One brain. The universal brain.

Osip That's so much "Volodya."

Mayakovsky A mega-god, who rules the world. Jehovah. Christ.

Osip Volodya—

Mayakovsky	Volodya what? Don't condescend to me. You act like a dumb-bell. Can't you follow what I'm saying?
Osip	Yes. We have the State, and the Church.
Mayakovsky	They're obsolete. We need brains only.
Osip	Are you drunk?
Mayakovsky	Don't ask me things like that, Osip. They infuriate me. Do I look drunk to you?
Osip	No, you never look drunk. But I'll bet your liver looks solid yellow.
Mayakovsky	You're on. How would we know?
Osip	Never mind. I don't want to bet.
Mayakovsky	Brains without substance. Brains that are brains only.
Osip	Like souls?
Mayakovsky	Yes, like souls.
Osip	Do we not have that now?
Mayakovsky	No, we don't have that now. Now we are fragile and die. We get sick and old and die. We die young. And the brain dies with us. What if the brain were independent, free of the body?
Osip	You'd need a wire.
Mayakovsky	A wire?
Osip	I'm sorry. Bad joke.
Mayakovsky	Free of the body and connected to the others, like a spiritual force scanning the universe.
Osip	That *is* the universe. Transcendence.
Mayakovsky	No, I'm talking about a super substance, Osip.
Osip	So am I.
Mayakovsky	No, that's old. That's not true anymore.

Osip	Too much imagination, Volodya. And drink.
Mayakovsky	Go away, Osip, and let me ponder.
Osip	No. You're not well. I'll stay.
Mayakovsky	Leave me alone.
Osip	No.
Mayakovsky	Go and come back. Bring Lilyana.
Osip	Yes. I'll bring her.

A moment. Mayakovsky lies in his messy bed, gripping his neck and making flutish sounds through his nose. He is 36 years old. He imagines that he's lived 13 lives already. More than he deserves. He tried to write about each of them once, but never got further than a vague childhood. Once, he wanted to write about the women in his life. The many women, each in her turn. But he never got around to it. He found the biology humiliating, the beauty of women annihilating. He might have put it that way himself. Meanwhile he's telling you, through me, of what he knows are the existential horrors oppressing poets throughout time.

Scene 31

Nadja retrieves the little Mauser from underneath the embroidered yellow pillow and lies down with it on her chest. We are not there, of course. Nadja sighs a quiet breath. No one heard it then, no one hears it now. A muffled shot from the Mauser. A moment of quiet, as though, as they say, the air went out of the room.

Scene 32

*Osip comes back to Mayakovsky with Lily. Volodya
is on an entirely new project: the meaning of
exactitude.*

Mayakovsky   Lily. Osip. Listen. You're not paying attention. I'm
talking about the EXACT MOMENT. Exactly. On that
moment and not before. That precise moment, or
everything fails.

Lily   Fails? What does he mean?

Osip   I don't know.

Mayakovsky   The moment of Being, of existence itself. Full.
Complete.

Osip   The moment of exactly.

Mayakovsky   Yes, that's it. Precisely. The whole moment, and only
then. You see?

Osip   No.

Mayakovsky   Too little, too late. Too soon, too early. On time. The
exact whole moment.

Osip   I wasn't good at mathematics.

Mayakovsky   You are a peddler, Osip.

Lily   You must say what you mean, Volodya.

Mayakovsky   I am saying what I mean. There is an exact moment, a
whole note, when the gong is struck. Otherwise, there
are fragments, only fragments. The whole note has not
been struck, and so it flies apart. There is an exactitude
required that you have not encountered before,
darlings.

Lily   Let him sleep.

Mayakovsky	I don't need sleep. You fail to understand what I'm talking about. Understanding is what I need.
Osip	You need sleep, Volodya.
Mayakovsky	Go away. I'll rest now.
Lily	Good. *(A gunshot)*

Mayakovsky is dead as a doornail, his Mauser on his chest, grimacing at the ceiling, devils all around him taking photos. I look at the body—it is a photo of the body—it's not the lover boy, the avant-garde poet of the Revolution—not even him, it's light and shadow in a frame. A bloody splotch on the left side of his heart. Disheveled. Mouth open, darkness within, a maw of darkness. Crumpled tie around his neck. One can see the tragic loss of being, lost long ago. No perfection in the Soviet man. A huge fuss as the photographers rush in, along with Lily and Osip, and the rest of the Mayakovsky coterie. Everyone has that look: "It's a shame, but what can you do? The man was an adolescent."

Scene 33

Nadja lies on the bed. Blood seeps from her chest into the sheets. The earth moves inexorably on. Nothing, moving right along. The uniforms and tablecloths, haversacks and guns.
Later, as we all know, Stalin will nearly destroy the Russian Army and murder all of his friends, including one of his oldest friends, Kirov, the comrade who stuck

with him until the moment of his (Kirov's) dying at the hands of the secret police.

Really, we don't know. I wasn't born yet. My teen-age mother was working in a garment sweatshop in Brooklyn. My father had already broken his head by falling off a building.

After Nadja's suicide, Stalin didn't speak for weeks.

THE END

Afterword

An interview with Murray Mednick
by Gray Palmer

Murray Mednick and I had this conversation just after Mednick completed a draft of Mayakovsky and Stalin, *his kaleidoscopic set of personal perspectives near the Soviet leader, but more, a theatrical meditation on history-making. He had just moved to a new house in the San Fernando Valley. In our phone conversations beforehand, Mednick was in a retrospective mood, which delighted me, and was my cue to ask him questions that might shed light on how his craft developed. The conversation lasted for about an hour and is lightly edited—mostly to remove my delinquent assertiveness.*

Murray Mednick's first play, The Box, *is a monologue, and was directed at Theatre Genesis by Lee Kissman in 1965. Mednick brought the material to one of the Monday night readings at St. Mark's Church-in-the-Bowery. Many plays quickly followed.*

In April 1968, The Hawk, *his downtown success, moved from Theatre Genesis to the Actors' Playhouse uptown— and closed after 15 performances. In the* Times, *Clive Barnes wrote that "[It must signify] an awful lot that I could only dimly begin to understand . . ." We can take that as a critic's confession. Barnes was unable, in time for deadline, to articulate a message "fit-to-print" from the play. Other journal critics were "angry and bewildered," a pattern that continues to the present. (And the methods used to devise* The Hawk *were not so different from the methods used later, in California, for portions of* The Coyote Cycle—*as Mednick relates during this interview.)*

Did St. Mark's Church-in-the-Bowery, where he discovered his vocation, have something like a secret door that connected poets and playwrights? Maybe. Aspects of Mednick's theater can be thought of as something like animated calligrammes, Apollinaire's delightful late inventions. And the Poetry Project started at St. Mark's in 1966. Alice Notley said that for a long time she wrote for the poets in that room—was Mednick present?

In 1970, he received an Obie for his three-act play, The Deer Kill.

Prizes are all right if you get one, though it's always good to bear in mind who gives them. Jack Kroll, John Lahr, and the wicked John Simon were on the awards committee that year. Mednick was recognized along with the playwrights Joe Orton, Paul Zindel, Megan Terry, and Vaclav Havel. (Genesis-based actor Lee Kissman also received a 1970 Obie—for his performance in Sam Shepard's The Unseen Hand).

What happened in Mednick's work between 1965 and 1970? A compass-setting, I think.

Mednick has said, "[We found that] you could use a certain kind of visual symbology . . . to great effect in a small space. We were really interested in discovering iconographic usages: What would have the resonance of an icon, a newly discovered icon, so that you could communicate directly to the audience's subconscious?"

Spare visual presentation, and focus on the sequence of language.

I visited Mednick at his new house on a hot day in October 2016, just as Open Fist was preparing their ambitious production of The Gary Plays. *(Under the direction of Guy Zimmerman, they were presenting three full-length evenings culled from the cycle's eight plays.) We sat in his living room; beyond a glass door was his bright swimming pool—the light and composition was like a Hockney picture. Mednick spoke quietly.*

"Certain things can only be heard onstage"—Theater Poetry and the Chorus

Gray Palmer
What is theater poetry?

Murray Mednick
Yes. Well, first of all, it's rhythmic. And one's rhythms are of course one's own. Like Beckett's rhythms are a little different than Pinter's. But they're basically coming from the idea that the text is what's important. That's the unifying idea about poetry in the theater. The text comes first. Because all the actor's choices should derive from the sound and the movement and the rhythm and the textual implications, you know, the meaning of the text. Usually what happens is actors make interpretive and performative choices *before* they learn the text, *before* they know the text, before they've *heard* the text. So, that's a really important point . . . And then, poetry is, in a sense, it's a valuation of language. So, you can have what we call prose, it can be in that category, as long as it's carefully written and the writing is what's important and foremost. Not prosaic, let's say. Not necessarily realistic, even. That's what happens so often in the business and in entertainment. People are talking naturalistically, and the acting is naturalistic, the behavior is naturalistic, and the writing is naturalistic. And if you have a very good ear, you can get away with it and call it "poetic." But what makes it really poetic is that you're not stuck with trying to be realistic with the language, with character and plot—trying to catch the way people talk—then discoveries can be made. The aim is not just to catch the way people talk. It's what comes before, what comes after, where it's going. There's a kind of inner rhyming. And there's rhyming in the

text—unexpectedly. And then there's the sheer enjoyment of language and wit.

GP
By "rhyme" you mean something other than the repetition of terminal sound—The rhyme of event?

MM
Yes. And the rhyming of theme. Of phrases and ideas.

GP
What about the rhyme of behavior?

MM
I tend to suppress behavior as much as possible in favor of the text. Because actors have come to depend too much on behavior. Because in television behavior is the thing that carries the performance. Everything is according to, or dependent on, behavior. In a good actor, it's ok, I mean one doesn't mind that. But in the theater it's not that important. Language, speaking, is what's important. So, behavior tends to interfere. And I tend to discourage or minimize behavior when I direct.

GP
I know.

MM
You should know. But I like the movement to be crisp and choreographed.

GP
A picture that changes when the units of the play change.

MM

That's right, and it has to be coherent and precise. But that's me. Some people don't get into that too much. To me that's part of the poetry of the text, the corresponding movement, the transitions . . . They're just hard to do. Takes lots of repetition.

GP

The transitions are where you get the most arresting visual experience.

MM

Yes. They are visual moments. And there shouldn't be too much visual, besides that, going on. Except we've learned to use screens very well in my plays, just learned it almost by accident. But there's a place when you have—the kind of language I use—there's a natural place for imagery, if it's intentional. I mean projections, like in *Villon*. And they work really well in my plays. I'm not sure why, exactly. It has to do with the kind of writing it is. The writing doesn't demand a lot of visual aid. So, there's room for, if someone's really good at it, for corresponding projections that can be thematic and engaging. But indirectly. And that's interesting . . . Because the emphasis in my work is on the sound, there's room for an indirect, thematic progression of images . . . Of course, you don't think about that when you're writing . . . It's very interesting to me technically, and that's what gets me going, usually, to see if something will work. Like with the chorus idea, using the chorus as part of the text.

GP

What does a chorus mean?

MM

I was experimenting with what it means. The impulse came from wanting more voice, as the writer, to somehow be heard. So, it was kind of an inner chorus. So that the text would be going along and at certain points you'd hear an interjection . . . An inner voice. And the voice is authorial, in some cases. It's coming from the author. It's commentary. And that led to experimenting with the idea of the chorus in other ways. In *The Gary Plays*, in each play there's a different use of the chorus, another version . . . *Charles' Story* was the last of it. Although I still use the technique—I still use it—I have a play I'm thinking of, called *Mayakovsky and Stalin* . . .

GP

Mayakovsky would take any assignment they gave him.

MM

Yeah. He wrote a lot, he overwrote. He came to a bad end . . . He's sort of parallel with Stalin in the play. But I use a version of the chorus there that's a little different from *The Gary Plays*. As a kind of Narrator. Works nicely.

GP

You wrote *Tirade for Three*, the first of *The Gary Plays*, without attribution of voices.

MM

Yeah, the first version . . . Because it was so voice-oriented, I thought at the time that it would be interesting, in rehearsal, for the actors to find which lines they wanted to say. I thought it didn't matter, in a way. Because it was one whole, in a way, poetically. Except, when there was attribution, in the play, then they would step out of that mode and into a more usual dialogue format. More formal. But I thought when it was not in that format, it didn't matter, because the voices would speak for themselves. In the end the entire thing would find its own *metier*, you know, its own format. And I think it can still be done that way. It would depend a lot on the director. That's one way to go. Ultimately, I decided to attribute.

GP
At Electric Lodge in 2005, it seems to me, what you're describing, that was the way it was staged.

MM
Yes. That's the way it was done there . . .

Theatre Genesis and Ralph Cook

GP
At Theatre Genesis you worked with Ralph Cook.

MM
I'd love to tell you about him. I've been thinking about him lately. For example, all this emphasis about text, and the text being the important way into a play—I learned that from Ralph . . . I was a poet on the Lower East Side. I was also a waiter—and other things. One of my friends at the time was an actor named Warren Finnerty, a very good actor. He was in *Easy Rider*—the guy at the gas station. He since has gone, of blessed memory. He took me over to Theatre Genesis one night and I saw a couple of plays there. That's how I got into the theater. I saw a play called *The Inspector in Baggy Pants* by Lawrence Ferlinghetti. That was Ralph's idea—Ralph was very

interested in poetry for the theater, in poets writing for the theater. And so, he got poets like me interested. He said to me, "Just write something for the stage and I'll do it." So. He really would do it. He had made a program on Monday nights of readings of new plays. And you'd get these good actors down there. It became a thing, these Genesis Monday night readings, so you'd get to hear your work read by good actors. That's how I learned. Because I never went to school about theater—or anything like that. But I learned at Genesis. I learned about how it sounded, how things worked. But I was still a poet. And you start writing for the stage space and for live speech . . . That's a thing in its own right. So that by the time I got to Padua and started doing the Padua Festival here, I had enough background to be able to teach what I had learned—in other words, you see the stage and you hear the dialogue from the stage, which is very different than television or movie dialogue. And certain things can only be heard onstage. They can only be heard onstage. There's a certain kind of thought that can only be heard through that medium . . . There's another level, above, that's invoked, or evoked, by the appearance of the stage as a medium, or vehicle, for a certain kind of experience . . . That's a special kind of thought. It's thought that has more than one resonation. This idea of levels of meaning is very important . . .

GP
You're making gestures that indicate a horizontal axis and a vertical axis.

MM
That's what should happen in a good play. Where both are going . . . It's the actor who is the—this was what Artaud was trying to

say—it's the actor who does that transmutation. It goes through him. In doing so, as you know, being an actor, you can accomplish a certain freedom inside, that is hard to get anywhere else, in any other way . . . It's a state of grace.

GP
Like grace in sports.

MM
When you're hot. I agree. Except there's a little more . . . It has mind . . . And the audience shares it, they can share in it, if the actors get there and the play is good . . . They share the tension—the intention—which becomes almost a physical force. Which is irreplaceable and live . . . That's what makes it more interesting, for me, than movies.

GP
Watching TV or watching movies is an act of private consumption. But in the theater a group subjectivity may be formed.

MM
That's right. There's a unity. That's a real unity. And that is part of the ritual—in that sense. Because there's only one thing happening. There's a focus of attention. We're lucky to be in the theater for that reason . . .

GP
You've been in Los Angeles since 1978.

MM
75 actually.

GP

Ok, 40 years in Los Angeles, choosing, I presume, not to have anything to do with movies and TV—

MM

I tried, actually. In fact, what got me out here was a gig with KCET. I was commissioned to write two plays for KCET, for *Visions*, it was on channel 28 then. They did both of them. One was called *Iowa* and the other was called *Blessings*. That's what got me into the Writers Guild. And then I did try to write screenplays. I did a couple of gigs. I just couldn't do it well. Because I don't think that way. I couldn't re-train.

GP

Theater poetry is a double ghetto. A perfect recipe for obscurity.

MM

You're out there. We're not part of the economy. Which is too bad. It's a shame that America doesn't support theater as well as it could . . . But you know, technically, there's a big difference between writing for the stage and writing for movies . . . Movies are more for a sequence of images. In plays it's a sequence of language, it's the sound, the linguistic music . . . Theater is not a spectacle. There are spectacles like circuses, pageants, and musicals on Broadway which are spectacular. But real theater, I think, is more for the ear and so the craft is different. Completely different. And the craft I learned, more or less by accident, through Ralph Cook and Theatre Genesis, was theater. And my head works that way, I listen for the sound and for the rhythm. Before I even know who is talking. Character comes later, usually . . . I usually get the lines before the people. I'm doing that now. I'm writing lines—I don't know who is talking yet. But it has a nice rhythm and a cadence. That tells me something's cooking, so I can go on with it. And sooner or later I find out who they are. It could be past characters, new characters. But I don't know yet . . . and then there's a kind of click, and I begin to know what it's about.

Ralph, you know, was a minister to the arts. Ralph Cook believed that there was something underneath a play, or hidden in a play, if it was written by a real poet, that had special meaning. It was a kind of Christianity, really. I'm realizing this in retrospect. He was hired [as a lay curate for the arts] by Allen [Rector Michael Allen of St. Mark's Church-in-the-Bowery]. He was a Christian man. That was an attribute of Ralph's. He had a, not a systematic, but a real— not a theological, but a spiritual approach, to what theater was about, and what the search for the meaning of things was about— through the writing of the local poets. A very interesting way to go. And I was a local poet who happened upon him through my friend, Warren Finnerty, who was acting in Ferlinghetti's play. And I was a fan of Ferlinghetti's and his poetry. I knew that whole group. I knew that scene. So, my first friends were poets and actors. On the Lower East Side. This was the 60s, early 70s. And that's where all my attitudes about theater were formed . . . my sense of . . . that the playwright can be the director, for example . . . was at Theatre Genesis then. He didn't mind, Ralph Cook . . . He *did* mind, actually, but he let us direct if we wanted to.

Padua Hills Workshop and Festival

MM
And at Padua, I thought it was important, central, that the playwrights direct. I'm a real believer in that.

So that a playwright learns about the theatrical event?

MM

And also that he has the privilege of making those final choices. That's really important. He has that right. And it ought to be his privilege. And [Maria] Irene Fornes always agreed with me about that. She always directed her own work. She was totally right about it. She was fantastic to work with. Irene was one of the most brilliant people I've ever known. And she had her own stylistic integrity. She was a poet, too . . . *Mud* is a great play. It's a great play. We did it at Padua, which she directed. John O'Keefe was in it. He played Henry. He was terrific. He's also a good director. And so is [John] Steppling. See, we had the advantage, at Padua, the four of us, being able to direct. And we knew how to talk about the theater. And we each had our own approach. But we could talk intelligently about it.

So, that made it a really excellent school. Cause it had all the sides that a good theater school needs: good teachers, plays that are being performed for an audience, a company of actors who could read the student plays, workshops, and maintaining a professional performance schedule. So, we had all those aspects going at once. But the essential, most important thing, is we had the four of us who could talk about the theater. So that those meetings we had about the student plays, there with the students, were of a very high level of intelligence . . . I miss that . . . Those were really good experiences. Saturdays. Once a week. We'd have workshops during the week.

GP

Fornes, Steppling, yourself, and O'Keefe.

MM

Yeah, and I'd hire four other people each year. There'd be eight teachers in all. But the four people I hired every year were us four. I was the artistic director, so I was there. But the three people I wanted there every year were Irene and the two Johns. So, we had that continuity . . . Steppling is usually right about what he says. And he was good at Padua. It was good to have those other voices there. And he could write well for the site-specific spaces. It was very interesting what we did in those days. I hope Padua survives in memory. It's very important, historically.

GP

The scripts are there.

MM

The scripts are there. And the students, you know, if they stay alive. I guess I've been thinking about a lot of that stuff lately . . .

Recognition

GP

You're the recipient of two Rockefeller Foundation grants.

MM

And a Guggenheim.

GP

And a Guggenheim Fellowship. Is there anything to say about that kind of support now?

MM

It was really important then. Oh, absolutely. Like I was saying, it's support, you know. Like at Genesis, we never had any money.

So . . . it made things really tough. I mean, we got used to it. We got used to doing minimal shit. You couldn't do much with cues. You couldn't pay the actors. You'd conceive and you'd write that way.

GP
Empty space plays?

MM
Black space plays. Black rooms. So, everything was minimalized. And we did write that way. But we wanted to cast well—couldn't pay the actors enough. So, we had to have a dedicated group of actors, which we did have, luckily. But they should have been paid more. And we should have been paid. I was working as a waiter. Maybe it's my age now and I've been through the mill. But, you know, I'm OK now . . . But it's very important that theater arts, especially the avant-garde, the experimental side, be supported. To live and make a living at what you do is morally right. It helps the morale. And it's very difficult if you're struggling with that all the time. Anyway, that's how I remember it. We were always up against it. And gradually we did start getting grants. The state and the city. Through Theatre Genesis. But the theater was getting a little money. And then I did get these grants. And they made a big difference because I could travel, and I could eat regularly and have a better place to live. On the Lower East Side, I was living in these slum dwellings, you know, two rooms, two and a half rooms, the sink was in the bathroom. It was rough.

And it was important recognition.

GP
And now?

MM

I would like to have, speaking for now, I would love some kind of sponsor, or some kind of theater that would take me on. I've been doing my own work and supporting my own work. And I'm not done. But I don't have the money to produce any more, especially now that I've moved to this place. I have a backlog of plays that I would love to do, that I can't quite do at the moment. 'Cause I'm more or less on my own. So it would be fantastic—support from somewhere, from the state, from the county, from the city, or from a person or a sponsor or a theater, that could help me just to get my plays on. I'm still writing, I'm still good, I'm still interested in what I'm doing. But I don't have as much opportunity . . . The economics here are harder now. See, we could do it on nothing, then, because we were younger and more willing. And the feeling—it was opening up, experimentally. We were learning by doing it. We didn't have too much to do with the uptown scene. So, we had freedom—and money didn't matter as much. But as you get older it starts to matter more. As you know. Things have got really expensive. Even to do an Off-Off-Broadway-type play. Fifty thousand, at least. A half-audience house . . . In New York, a good Off-Off-Broadway play could get houses, if word-of-mouth is good and reviews are good . . . You only get half-houses in LA. So, you can't make it that way. Never make your money back. Not in that venue. So, when you produce a play like that, or finance it, it's a give-away. You can write it off your taxes. But that's about it.

From the Family Series

GP

About your play *Joe and Betty*, the critic Bruce Weber said in the *New York Times* that it was a miracle the playwright survived his family.

MM

That's a very good way to put it . . . I kind of agree with that. But I think the play is exhilarating. It is grim, but it's exhilarating. Because of the language, because of the way it moves. I'm using vaudevillian rhythms. But it's grim. No, it's not comedy. And it was tough, that way. But it was very true to life. And it caught the rhythms . . . I was trying to be conscientious about that. I didn't want to be too negative . . . It was grimmer than that, though, in real life . . . It was more traumatic than I wanted to make it in the play . . . Delight is in the music . . . Vaudeville is a main influence on me, I think.

GP

How did that happen?

MM

I don't know how it happened. I grew up partly in the Catskills. Spent time growing up there, so I saw a lot of stand-up. The rhythms and the vaudevillian timing. In a way it's about timing, it's all in the timing . . . Jack Benny was one of my idols . . . I'm sure Pinter was influenced by the duo acts in English Music Hall. So was Beckett. Music Hall stuff. I was just more on the Yiddishkeit element. And I like that play very much, *Joe and Betty*, although it gives me a twinge.

The Coyote Cycle

GP

To write *The Coyote Cycle*, did you read ethnographic material?

MM

Yeah, I did. I read a lot of Indian stuff. But I've always been into the American Indian story. And I admire a lot of their world. And we got a lot of support from the indigenous community. That was magical. We did some ceremonies with Leonard Crow Dog, for example. And most of the stuff in *The Coyote Cycle* is authentic Indian mystic material. The stories are all Native American. Old Nana was an Apache. I knew a lot about it. And I invented the exercises. And based several of the plays on exercises. Some of the plays were written on-the-spot through exercises with the actors.

GP

Norbert Weisser and Darrell Larson.

MM

We started at my backyard in La Verne, California. Darrell and Norbert and I started doing these exercises. That first one I took from Carlos Castaneda. Finding the Spot. Don Juan tells Carlos: find the spot that's meaningful to you. That's your spot. So, I adapted and took theater exercises, with Darrell and Norbert, like Finding the Spot, and then demonstrating its meaning to you through sound and movement. And then we started finding postures. Pointing and the Defensive Posture. That's what made the play . . . And I wrote it as poetry, really. *Pointing*, the first play in *The Coyote Cycle*, it's a poem, and it did beautifully . . . A priceless thing . . . Norbert . . . he's a class-A actor. So is Darrell . . . The two of them were great with me. We did all seven together. When Priscilla Cohen came in as Clown, and Christine Avila, the second year, as Spider Woman, joined us, that was the basic company. Some of the plays I wrote beforehand. And some I did based on the exercises, or the spot, the site.

GP

You perform the seven plays all together.

MM

Twilight to dawn is they way they were meant to be done, outside, seven different sites, twilight to dawn. And with a waterfall. So, wherever we went, when we did the all-night production, we built a waterfall. It was fantastic. Those cues are unbeatable, like Trickster erupting from the Earth. So, the last thing that would happen, we'd come to the end, and these guys are all taking these postures that I gave them, and the sun is coming up and the waterfall is coming down. It's just great, an unbelievable gift, from the point of view of a theater-maker.

2019 Production Information

Mayakovsky and Stalin—Los Angeles
Produced by *Racquel Lehrman, Theater Planners*
Scenic & Projection Designer *Nick Santiago*
Costume Designer *Shon LeBlanc*
Lighting Designer *Matt Richter*
Sound Designer & Original Music *John Zalewski*
Assistant Producer *Misha Riley, Theater Planners* Racquel's credit
Casting Director *Raul Clayton Staggs*
Production Stage Manager *Danny Crisp*

Cast
Rhonda Aldrich *Yelena*
Daniel Dorr *Mayakovsky*
Max Faugno *Chorus*
Andy Hirsch *Osip*
Laura Liguori *Lily*
Casey McKinnon *Nadja*
Alexis Boozer Sterling *Elsa*
Maury Sterling *Stalin*
Ann Colby Stocking *Masha*
(Max Faugno, as the *Chorus*, also played *Kirov* and *Voroshilov*.)

Mayakovsky and Stalin—New York
Produced by *Racquel Lehrman, Theater Planners*
Scenic & Projection Designer *Hana S. Kim*
Costume Designer *Shon LeBlanc*
Lighting Designer *Pablo Santiago*
Sound Designer & Original Music *John Zalewski*

Assistant Producer *Misha Riley, Theater Planners*
Additional Casting *Michael Donovan, CSA*
Production Stage Manager *Danny Crisp*

Cast
Michelle Azar *Masha*
Jennifer Cannon *Nadja*
Daniel Dorr *Mayakovsky*
Max Faugno *Chorus*
Andy Hirsch *Osip*
Laura Liguori *Lily*
Alexis Boozer Sterling *Elsa*
Maury Sterling *Stalin*
(Max Faugno, as the *Chorus,* also played *Kirov* and *Voroshilov.*)

Guy Zimmerman The artistic director of Padua Playwrights in Los Angeles, Zimmerman's articles and essays about theater, film, art, and politics have been published in, among others, *Theater Journal*, *SubStance*, *Shakespeare Bulletin*, *TheaterForum*, *LA Weekly*, and in the arts and culture website *Times Quotidian*. Under his direction, Padua has staged more than fifty productions of new plays, moving several to stages in Atlanta, New York City, Edinburgh, Prague, Berlin, Beirut, and Cluj, Romania. His own plays include *La Clarita*, *The Inside Job*, *Vagrant*, *The Black Glass*, *The Hillary Game*, *The Royal*, and *Double Double* and his films include *Gary's Walk*, *Great Things*, *Pronghorn*, *The Wasps*, and *Hello, Say*.

Gray Palmer is a writer, director, and performer based in Los Angeles. His play *Plan B* was published in the anthology *I Might Be the Person You Are Talking To* from Padua Press. His theater journalism can be found online in the archives of *Stage Raw*.

Murray Mednick is the founder of the Padua Hills Playwrights Festival and Workshop, where he served as Artistic Director from 1978 through 1995. Born in Brooklyn in 1939, he was for many years a playwright-in-residence at New York's Theatre Genesis, which presented much of his early work, including *The Hawk*, *The Deer Kill*, *The Hunter*, *Sand*, and *Are You Lookin'?* He was artistic co-director of Theatre Genesis from 1970 to 1974, when he emigrated to California. Plays produced since then include *Iowa* and *Blessings* (for the PBS series *Visions*), *The Coyote Cycle*, *Taxes*, *Scar*, *Heads*, *Shatter 'n Wade*, *Fedunn*, *Switchback*, *Baby Jesus!*, *Dictator*, *Freeze*, *16 Routines*, *Mrs. Feuerstein*, *G-nome*, and *Joe and Betty*.

Mednick is the recipient of two Rockefeller Foundation grants, a Guggenheim Fellowship, an OBIE, several Bay Area Critics Awards, and a 1992 Ovation Lifetime Achievement Award from Theater LA for outstanding contributions to Los Angeles theater. He won the 1997 (*Dictator*) and 2003 (*Fedunn*) *L.A. Weekly* Playwriting Awards. His play *Joe and Betty* received the 2002 American Theater Critics Association Best New Play Citation. Mednick was awarded the 2002 Margaret Harford Award for Sustained Excellence in Theater by the Los Angeles Drama Critics Circle, and in the same year, a career achievement award from the *L.A. Weekly*.